The Eight-Step Path
of Policy Analysis
A Handbook for Practice

The Eight-Step Path
of Policy Analysis

A Handbook for Practice

by Eugene Bardach

Berkeley Academic Press
Berkeley

First Edition

Cover design by: Nathan Neely

Library of Congress Catalog Card Number: 96-85903
ISBN: 0-9652903-0-1

Berkeley Academic Press
Berkeley

P.O. Box 4900, Berkeley, CA 94704
Phone (510) 534-3434 • Fax (510) 534-1781

Preface

This is a handbook of concepts and methods for working your way through a policy analysis. The presumed user is a beginning practitioner preparing to undertake a policy analysis. I have developed the general approach and many of the specific suggestions over twenty years of teaching policy analysis workshops to first- and second-year graduate students at the Graduate School of Public Policy, University of California, Berkeley. I have also found this handbook useful in teaching an undergraduate introduction to public policy and for executive education groups.

The handbook assumes a familiarity with basic economic concepts, including those having to do with "market failures" ("market imperfections"). It is not meant to stand alone but should be used in conjunction with other sources. Four of the best textbooks in policy analysis which amplify points in this handbook are:

— Edith Stokey and Richard Zeckhauser, *A Primer for Policy Analysis*, W. W. Norton, 1978.

— David L. Weimer and Aidan R. Vining, *Policy Analysis: Concepts and Practice*, Prentice Hall, 1992.

— Robert D. Behn and James W. Vaupel, *Quick Analysis for Busy Decision-Makers*, Basic Books, 1982.

— Lee S. Friedman, *Microeconomic Policy Analysis*, McGraw Hill, 1984.

I wish to acknowledge the patience of, and the helpful reactions from, all the students and friends who have made use of this handbook, especially those who put up with its earlier versions. Special thanks are due to José Canela, John Ellwood, Nina Goldman, David Kirp, Leo

Levenson, Martin A. Levin, Duncan MacRae, Carolyn Marzke, Michael O'Hare, Andres Roemer, Larry Rosenthal, Mark Sabean, Eugene Smolensky, and David Weimer.

The Eight-Step Path

Part I
The Eight-Step Path

Introduction

Policy analysis is a social and political activity. True, you take personal moral and intellectual responsibility for the quality of your policy analytic work. But policy analysis goes beyond personal decision-making. First, the subject matter concerns the lives and well-being of large numbers of our fellow citizens. Secondly, the process and results of policy analysis usually involve other professionals and interested parties: it is often done in team or office-wide settings; the immediate consumer is a "client" of some sort like a hierarchical superior; and the ultimate audience will include diverse subgroups of politically attuned supporters and opponents of your work. All of these facts condition the nature of policy analytic work and have a bearing on the nature of what is meant by "quality" work.

Policy analysis—more art than science

Policy analysis is more art than science. It draws on intuition as much as method. Nevertheless, given the choice between advice that imposes too much structure on the problem-solving process and too little, most beginning practitioners quite reasonably prefer too much. I have therefore developed an approach I call "the eight-step path." The primary utility of this structured approach is that it reminds you of important tasks and choices that otherwise might slip your mind; its primary drawback is that, taken by itself, it can be mechanistic.

The Eight-Step Path

Define the Problem

Assemble Some Evidence

Construct the Alternatives

Select the Criteria

Project the Outcomes

Confront the Tradeoffs

Decide!

Tell Your Story

Iterate

These steps are not necessarily taken in precisely this order, nor is each one necessarily significant in every problem. However, an effort to *define the problem* is almost always the right starting place, and *telling your story* is almost inevitably the ending point. *Constructing alternatives* and *selecting criteria* for evaluating them must surely come towards the beginning of the process. *Assembling some evidence* is actually a step that recurs throughout the entire process, and applies particularly to efforts to *define the problem* and to *project the outcomes* of the alternatives being considered.

Iteration is continual

The problem-solving process—being a process of trial-and-error—is iterative, so that you usually must repeat each of these steps, sometimes more than once.

The spirit in which you take any one of these steps, especially in the earliest phases of your project, should be highly tentative. As you move through the problem-solving process, you will probably keep changing your problem definition, your menu of alternatives, your set of evaluative criteria, your sense of what evidence bears on the problem, and so on. With each successive iteration you will become a bit more confident that you are "on the right track," "focussing on the right question," etc. This can be a frustrating process; but it can also be rewarding—provided you can learn to enjoy the challenge of search, discovery, and invention.

Some of the guidelines are practical, but most are conceptual

Most of the concepts used below will seem obvious. However, there are exceptions. First, technical terms are sometimes employed. Second, some common-sense terms may be used in a special way that strips them of certain connotations and perhaps imports others. For the most part, all these concepts will become intelligible through experience and practice.

The concepts come embedded in concrete particulars

In real life, policy problems appear as a confusing welter of details: personalities, interest groups, rhetorical demands, budget figures, legal rules and interpretations, bureaucratic routines, citizen attitudes, and so on. Yet the concepts described in this handbook are formulated in the abstract. You therefore need to learn to "see" the analytic concepts in the concrete manifestations of everyday life.

A concluding sketch

So what will your final product look like? Here is a very rough sketch of a typical written policy analytic report: In a coherent narrative style you will describe some problem that needs to be mitigated or solved; you will lay out a few alternative courses of action which might be taken; to each course of action you will attach a set of projected outcomes that you think your client or audience would care about, suggesting the evidentiary grounds for your projections; if no alternative dominates all other alternatives with respect to all the evaluative criteria of interest, you will indicate the nature and magnitude of the tradeoffs implicit in different policy choices; depending on the client's expectations, you might state your own recommendation as to which alternative should be chosen.

I. Define the Problem

Your first problem definition is a crucial step. It gives you (1) a reason for doing all the work necessary to complete the project, and (2) a sense of direction for your evidence-gathering activity. And in the last phases of the policy analysis, your final problem definition will probably help you structure how you *tell your story*.

p.57
N.B.

Usually, the raw material for your initial problem definition comes from your client, and derives from the ordinary language of debate and discussion in the client's political environment, language I call generically "issue rhetoric." This rhetoric may be narrowly confined to a seemingly technical problem or broadly located in a controversy of wide social interest. In either case, you have to get beneath the rhetoric to define a problem that is analytically manageable and that makes sense in light of the political and institutional means available for mitigating it.

Use the raw material of issue rhetoric with care. It often points to some condition of the world that people don't like or consider "bad" in some sense, like "teenage pregnancy," "media violence," or "global warming." These evaluations do not necessarily need to be taken at face value. You will sometimes wish to explore the philosophical and empirical grounds on which you, your client, or others in your eventual audience should or should not consider the alleged condition "bad." Furthermore, issue rhetoric may point to some alleged— but not necessarily real—cause of the troubling condition, e.g., "welfare" or "human wastefulness." You do not want to simply echo the issue rhetoric in your problem definition, but to use it as raw material for a provisional problem definition that you hope will prove analytically useful.

Some issues may connote more than one problem. Depending on the audience, for example, "teenage pregnancy" might connote: sexual immorality, the blighting of young people's and their children's life chances, exploitation of taxpayers, or social disintegration. Usually you will want to determine a primary problem focus—otherwise you will find that the analysis gets out of hand. But if the problems aren't too complicated, you may feel you are willing to define more than one.

Think of "deficits" and "excesses"

It often—but not always—helps to think in terms of deficit and excess. For instance: "There are too many homeless people in the United States," or "The demand for agricultural water is growing faster than our ability to supply it at an acceptable financial and environmental cost" or "California's population of school-age children is growing at 140,000 per year, and our ability to develop the physical facilities in which to educate them is not growing nearly as fast."

It often helps to include the word "too" in the definition, e.g., "too big," "too small," "growing too slowly," "growing too fast." These last two phrases remind us that problems deserving our attention don't necessarily exist today but are in prospect for the future, whether near or distant.

However, it does not help to think in terms of deficit and excess when "the problem" is either (1) making a decision between well-structured alternatives ("Dump the dredging spoils in the Bay or somewhere out in the Pacific Ocean?") or (2) finding any way to accomplish some defined objective ("Raise grant funds to close the anticipated gap between revenues and expenditures").

The definition should be evaluative

Remember the idea of "a problem" usually means that people think there is something wrong with the world.

But note that "wrong" and "undesirable" are very debatable terms. Not everyone will think that the facts you (or others) have defined as a problem are "really" a problem, for each person may apply a different evaluative framework to these facts. Unfortunately, there are no obvious or accepted ways to resolve philosophical differences of this type.

A common philosophical as well as practical question is, "What private troubles warrant definition as public problems and thereby legitimately raise claims for amelioration by public resources?" It is almost always helpful to view the situation through the market failure lens.[1] When markets are working reasonably well, it is hard for government to intervene without creating important inefficiencies in the economy, inefficiencies which would likely make the sum of private troubles even greater than they were previously. Of course, since there are many important values besides economic efficiency, and since we sometimes choose to worsen some people's grievances in order to ameliorate those of others, we may sometimes wish to intervene even when markets are thought to be working well.

Quantify if possible

The definition should, insofar as possible, include a quantitative feature, that is, include magnitudes. How big is "too big"? How small is "too small"? How about "too slowly"? How about "too fast"? In the examples

---

1. See Weimer and Vining, chapter 3.

above, how many homeless people?*How many acre-feet of water are used now, and how does that compare with the demand in some specified future year (given certain assumptions about water pricing)? Exactly what is "our ability to develop physical facilities" and how do we expect it to grow, or shrink, over time?

If necessary, gather information to help you calibrate the relevant magnitudes. See the discussion below on "Assemble Some Evidence."

p.13

In many or most cases you will have to estimate—or "guesstimate," more likely—the magnitudes in question. Sometimes you should furnish a range as well as a point estimate of magnitudes. ("Our best guess of the number of homeless persons in families is 70,000, although it certainly lies somewhere between 40,000 and 130,000.")

Conditions that cause problems are also problems

Some problem conditions are not experienced as troublesome per se by citizens but are perceived by them, or by analysts working on their behalf, to be causes of troubles. It is sometimes useful to diagnose one or more alleged causes of this type and to define these as problems to be mitigated or removed. For instance, "One of the problems in the air pollution area is that states have not been willing to force motorists to keep their engines tuned up and their exhaust systems in proper order." In order to define problems of this causal type, you may need to engage in fairly strenuous social scientific analysis—see "Project the Outcomes" for further discussion.

p.36

Missing an opportunity is a problem

A special case of "a problem" is an opportunity missed. Is it not rather small-minded to think of policy analysis as devoted merely to the amelioration of "problems"? May policy analysis not rise above the tedious and uninspiring business of patching and fixing? Can we not aspire to a world in which we can identify opportunities to do creative—not to say "wonderful"—things? "If it ain't broke, don't fix it," is a confining idea, and certainly policy analysts, policy-makers, and public managers ought not to allow the "problem" focus to restrict the search for plausible opportunities. Unfortunately, the working agenda of most policy professionals is set by complaints, threats, worries, and troubles. There is often little time or energy left over to think about improvements which no one has identified as possible.

Where do we find opportunities for creative policy improvements that haven't first been identified by complaints, threats, etc.? Little academic or technical theory is available to answer this question. But, by way of examples, Appendix A notes some generic opportunities that are often just lying about, waiting to be exploited.

p.67

Common pitfalls in problem definition

DEFINING THE SOLUTION INTO "THE PROBLEM." Your problem definition should not include an implicit solution introduced by semantic carelessness. Keep the problem definition stripped down to a mere description, and leave open where you will look for solutions.

— Don't say: "There is too little shelter for homeless families." This formulation might inadvertently imply that "more shelter" is the best solution, and might inhibit you from thinking about ways to prevent them from "becoming homeless" in the first place. Try instead: "There are too many homeless families."

— Don't say: "New schools are being built too slowly." This formulation could imply "more schools" as the solution and could inhibit you from thinking about ways to use existing facilities more efficiently. Try instead: "There are too many schoolchildren relative to the currently available classroom space."

A tip-off that you're probably smuggling an implicit solution into the problem definition is to hear yourself saying, "Aha, but that's not the real problem; the real problem is..." While there are better and worse ways to conceptualize a problem, or to solve a problem, it stretches ordinary usage too much to say that one problem could be "more (less) real" than another.

Be skeptical about implicit causal claims. I said above that "conditions that cause problems are also problems." However, the causes must be real, not merely assumed. You have to evaluate the causal chain that goes from the situation itself to the bad things it is alleged to cause, and convince yourself that the causal chain is real. For instance, for some people, "cocaine use" is not a problem in itself, but it might be a problem if it leads to crime, poor health, family disintegration, etc. But does it lead to these outcomes, and to what degree? The evidence on this question should be evaluated very carefully before you decide it's okay to work with a problem definition involving "too much cocaine use."

↓Iterate

Problem-definition is a crucial step. But, because it is hard to get it right, you might take that same step again and again. Over the course of your analytic work, your empirical and conceptual understanding will evolve. Also, you begin to rule out alternative approaches to solving or mitigating your problem, and will probably want to sculpt the problem definition so that, in the end, you, and the political system, will have some chance of attacking the problem successfully. Finally, if you are working in an office or agency context, you will implicitly be negotiating a mutually acceptable problem-definition with your analyst colleagues and your hierarchical superiors.

II. Assemble Some Evidence

All of your time doing a policy analysis is spent in two activities: thinking (sometimes aloud and with others) and hustling data which can be turned into "evidence." Of these two activities, thinking is by far the more important (see discussion below on the value of social scientific research in "Project the Outcomes"), but hustling data takes by far the most time: reading documents, hunting in libraries, pouring over studies and statistics, interviewing people, traveling to interviews and waiting for appointments, and so on.

p.38

The real-world settings in which policy analysis is done rarely afford the time for a research effort that would please a careful academic researcher. In fact, "time pressure" is as dangerous an enemy of high-quality policy analysis as politically motivated bias, if not more so. Therefore it is essential to economize on your data-collection activities. The key to economizing is this: try to collect only those data that can be turned into "information" which, in turn, can be converted into "evidence" that has some bearing on your problem.

For the logically-minded, here are some definitions. "Data" are facts—or some might say, representations of facts—about the world. Data include all sorts of statistics but go well beyond statistics, too. Data also include, for instance, facts about an agency manager's ability to deal constructively with the press. "Information" is data that has "meaning," in the sense that it can help you sort the world into different logical or empirical categories. "Evidence" is information that affects the existing beliefs of important people (including yourself) about significant features of the problem you are studying and how it might be solved or mitigated.

You need evidence for three principal purposes. One purpose is to assess the nature and extent of the problem(s) you are trying to define. The second is to assess the particular features of the concrete policy situation you are engaged in studying. For instance, you may need to know—or guess—about agency workloads, recent budget figures, demographic changes in a service area, the political ideology of the agency chief, the competency of the middle-level managers in the agency, and the current attitudes of some other agency which nominally cooperates with this one on some problem. The third purpose is to assess policies that have been thought, by at least some people, to have worked effectively in situations apparently similar to your own, in other jurisdictions, perhaps, or at other times. All three purposes are relevant to the goal of producing realistic projections of possible policy outcomes.

Because each of these purposes becomes salient in different phases of the policy analysis process, this step on the Eight-Step Path will be taken more than once, but with a different focus each time.

▼ Iterate

Think before you collect

Thinking and collecting data are complementary activities: you can be a much more efficient collector of data if you think, and keep on thinking, about what you do and don't need (or want) to know, and why. The principal—and exceedingly common—mistake made by beginners and veterans alike is to spend time collecting information that has no conceivable or even plausible analytic value.

THE VALUE OF INFORMATION. What is the evidentiary value of information? The answer may be cast in a decision-analytic framework ("decision trees"), though you should remember that the process of "making a decision" involves a great many elements prior to the moment of actual "choice," such as defining a useful problem, thinking up better candidate solutions, selecting a useful "model," etc. That is, in general, the value of information depends on:

— the likelihood that it will cause you to substitute some better decision for whatever decision you would have made without it (which might have been an "acceptable" decision in and of itself);

— the likelihood that the substituted decision will, directly or indirectly, produce a better policy outcome than the outcome that would have been produced by the original decision;

— the magnitude of the difference in value between the likely improved outcome and the original outcome.

SELF-CONTROL. A helpful check to avoid collecting useless data, is to ask yourself, before embarking on some data collection venture:

— "Suppose the data turn out to look like so-and-so as opposed to thus-and-such, what implication would that have for my understanding of how to solve this problem?"; and

— "Compared to my best guess about how the data will look once I've got them, how much different might they look if I actually took the trouble to get them?"; and

— "How much is it worth to me to confirm the actual difference between what I can guess and what I can learn about the world by really getting the data?".

It is this sort of critical attitude about the value of expensive data collection that often leads good and experienced policy analysts to make do with "back of the envelope" estimates. However, none of the above is meant to be an excuse for shirking the job of getting good data—and sometimes lots of it, at huge costs in time and money—when you've convinced yourself that the investment really would pay off. There's an obvious and critical difference between justifiable and unjustifiable "guesstimates."

Survey "best practice"

The chances are that the problem you are studying is not absolutely unique, and that policy-makers and public managers in other jurisdictions, perhaps not too different from the one you are studying, have dealt with it in some fashion. See if you can track down some of these past solutions, and see if you can extrapolate something from them for the situation you are studying.

Use analogies

Sometimes it pays to gather data about things that are, on the surface, quite unlike the problem you are studying but that, under the surface, show instructive similarities. For instance, if you are working on the problem of how the State of California can discipline, and perhaps disbar, incompetent attorneys, you might usefully spend a good deal of your time learning about how the medical profession handles problems of physician incompetency, and not only in California but in other jurisdictions (even nations) as well.

Start early

You are often dependent on the schedules of other very busy people whom you ask to furnish information or opportunities for interviews. It is extremely impor-

tant to put in requests for information, especially interviews, well in advance of when you expect to want to
have completed the information-collection.[1]

Touching base, gaining credibility, brokering consensus

The process of assembling evidence inevitably has a
political as well as a purely analytical purpose. Sometimes it entails touching base with potential critics of
your work so that they will not be able to complain that
you ignored their perspectives. By making yourself
known to potential supporters of your work, you may
also be able to create a cadre of defenders.

A more complex objective, where appropriate, might
be to blend policy analysis with the process of improving a policy idea or decision during the course of implementation. (See below, the discussion of "improvability"
as a criterion.) This entails obtaining "feedback" from
participants, usually in an iterative process, and shar-
ing some of your own reactions with them. You become
more of a partner in the process than an outside
observer and diagnostician. An even more complex and
challenging role is for you to become a particular type
of "partner," a facilitator and broker, whether by acting
as a transmission belt from one person to another or by
convening meetings and other gatherings.

p.32

----

1. For a useful description of how to conduct literature
reviews, library searches, phone interviews, and personal
interviews, see Weimer and Vining, Ch. 6A. Also Eugene Bardach, "Gathering Data for Policy Research," Part II of this
book.

III. Construct the Alternatives

By "alternatives" I mean something like "policy options," or alternative "courses of action," or alternative "strategies of intervention to solve or mitigate the problem."

Start comprehensive, end up focussed

In the last stages of your analysis, you won't want to be assessing more than three or four principal alternatives. But in the beginning, you should err on the side of comprehensiveness: Make a list of all the alternatives you might wish to consider in the course of your analysis. Later on you will discard some obvious losers, combine others, and reorganize still others into a single "basic" alternative with one or more subsidiary "variants." For your initial list, though, where should you turn for ideas?

— Note the alternatives that key political actors are actively proposing or seem to have on their mind. These may include people's pet ideas, institutions' inventories of "off-the-shelf" proposals that simply await a window of opportunity, and prepackaged proposals that political ideologues are perennially advocating.

— Try to invent alternatives that might prove to be superior to the alternatives currently being discussed by the key political actors. It's good to brainstorm, to try to be creative—though don't expect that you'll necessarily produce much better ideas than other people have already come up with. One way to coax your creativity is to refer to the checklist in Appendix B entitled "Things Governments Do." For each entry on the list, ask yourself "Might it make sense to try some version of

p.69

this generic strategy to help mitigate this problem?"[1] Because it is a long and comprehensive list, the answer with respect to any single strategy will usually be negative. But the list is not very long and, with experience, you will need to spend only a few minutes to decide whether any of the ideas might be worth considering further.

— Always include in your first approach to the problem the alternative "Take no action; let present trends continue undisturbed." You need to do this because the world is full of naturally occurring change and some of these ongoing changes might mitigate the problem on which you are working. (Note that I am not characterizing this alternative as "Do Nothing..." It is not possible to "do nothing." Most of the trends in motion will probably persist and alter the problem, whether for better or for worse.)

However, in most cases, this "let-present-trends-continue..." option will drop out of your final analysis. This happens because, if you do your problem definition work well, you will end up with a real and important problem in your sights that in most cases can be mitigated to some degree by doing something affirmative.

— Inspect the most common sources of "natural" change in the public policy environment to see if any will affect the scope of the problem:

a) Political changes following elections. Also, changes induced by the prospects of having to contest an election.

---

1. See also the very valuable discussion on generic policy instruments in Weimer and Vining, ch. 5.

The Eight-Step Path

b) Changes in unemployment and inflation rates that accompany the business cycle.

c) The changing "tightness" or "looseness" of agency budgets caused by overall taxing and spending policies.

d) Demographic changes such as population migration patterns and population "bulges" moving through certain age grades.

Analyze the causes of the problem

It will often be useful to ask, "Can we explicate some system that holds this problem in place or keeps it going?" In general, popular understanding of the causes of policy problems tends to overemphasize "bad personalities" and "bad motives." It usually takes us further, though, to think about problems as being embedded in some kind of system, e.g., a market that underprices certain goods, like clean air, or a bureaucratic agency that is bound by its own standard operating procedures, or a neighborhood in which crime, business withdrawal, job loss, and resident alienation form a vicious circle. (See also, below, *Project the Outcomes.*)

p.36

Logically, it is not necessary to know the causes of a problem in order to cure it—pharmaceutical manufacturers can testify that many of their successful products work by unknown causal routes on conditions whose causes are not at all understood. But a good causal schema is often quite useful for suggesting possible "intervention points." Consider, for instance, a system which produces "too much traffic congestion" at some choke point like a bridge or a tunnel. A sketch of the relevant causal system would include among other things the demand for travel along the relevant route, the available modes of travel, the amount of roadway capacity, and the price to users of roadway capacity. An efficient and simple—but usually politically unpopular—intervention might be to increase the price to users of the capacity so as to reflect the degree to which each user contributes to congestion and increased travel times.

Reduce and simplify the list of alternatives

The final list of alternatives—the one you include in your presentation to your client and other audiences—will almost certainly look quite different from the one you started with. Not only will you have thrown some out that just don't look very good, but you will have done some work to conceptualize and simplify alternatives.

The key to conceptualizing is to try to sum up the basic strategic thrust of an alternative in a simple sentence or even phrase. This is difficult but usually worth the effort. It usually helps to use very plain, short phrases stripped of jargon. When the EPA was first created, the first Administrator confronted (a partial list of) alternatives that might have been described thus: "Let the states do the work—let the feds give them the money"; "Remove impediments to firms cooperating on anti-pollution research"; "Sue the bastards" (meaning the large, visible polluting firms and industries, the prosecution of which would help build political support for the new agency).

The key to simplification is to distinguish between a "basic" alternative and its "variants." The "basic" element in many policy "alternatives" is an "intervention strategy," such as regulatory enforcement or a subsidy or a tax incentive, that causes people or institutions to change their conduct in some way. But no intervention strategy can stand alone: it must be implemented by some agency or constellation of agencies (perhaps including nonprofit organizations); and it must have a source of financing. Usually the "variants" on the basic strategy include different methods of implementation and different methods of financing.

The distinction between "basic" strategy and "variants" based on implementation details is especially helpful when you have a lot of possible solutions to consider and you need to reduce the complexity involved in comparing them. Making the distinction puts you in a position to break your analysis into successive steps. In the first step you might compare three "basic" alternatives, say, while ignoring the details described by their "variants." Then, once you had decided on one of these "basic" alternatives, you would turn to comparing the "variants." Here are two examples:

— You want to decrease the prevalence of heroin use in your county by 50% over the next five years. You consider three "basic approaches": methadone maintenance, law enforcement pressure, and drug education. Variants for each one have to do with the funding sources, in that state, federal, and county monies can be used in different degrees (although not all mixes of funds available for one approach are also available for the other two). Variation is also possible according to who administers the program(s): nonprofit organizations, county employees, state employees.

— You can also consider "variants" of scale and scope. In the above example, you might wish to consider two possible sizes for your methadone program, for instance.

A linguistic pitfall

"Alternative" does not necessarily signify that the policy options are mutually exclusive. Among policy analysts the term "alternative" is used ambiguously. Sometimes it means that choosing one implies foregoing another; and somctimcs it means simply one more policy action that might help solve or mitigate some problem, perhaps in conjunction with other "alternatives." You should be aware of the ambiguity in other people's usage and, in *telling your story* (Step Eight), you should be sure that no such ambiguity enters your own usage.

p.60

N.B.

Sometimes you won't be entirely sure whether two alternatives are or are not mutually exclusive. For instance, the mayor earlier might have promised enough money to either fix potholes or provide homeless shelters (but not both); but you may have made such a great case for both programs that the mayor might decide to increase the budgetary allocation.

IV. Select the Criteria

It helps to think of any policy story (see Step Eight) as having two interconnected but separable plot lines, the analytical and the evaluative. The first is all about ![p.59 arrow] p.59 N.B. facts and disinterested projections of consequences, while the second is all about value judgments. Ideally, all analytically sophisticated and open-minded persons should be able to agree, more or less, on the rights and wrongs in the analytical plot and on the nature of its residual uncertainties. But this is not true with regard to the evaluative plot—where we expect subjectivity and social philosophy to cavort more freely. The analytical plot will reason about whether X, Y, or Z is likely to happen, but it is in the evaluative plot that we learn whether we think X, Y or Z good or bad for the world.

The step in the Eight-Step Path called *Select the criteria* belongs to the evaluative plot line. It is the most important step for permitting values and philosophy to be brought into the policy analysis, because "criteria" are evaluative standards used to judge the "good-ness" of the projected policy outcomes associated with each of the alternatives.

Apply criteria to judging outcomes, not alternatives

Please note that criteria are not used to judge the alternatives, or at least not directly. They are to be applied to the projected outcomes. It is easy to get confused about this point—and to get the analysis very tangled as a result. This confusion is encouraged by a common-sense way of speaking: "Alternative A looks to be the best—therefore let's proceed with it." But this way of speaking ignores a very important step. The complete formulation is: "Alternative A very probably leads to outcome O_A, which we judge to be the best of the possible outcomes; therefore, we judge alternative A to be the best." Applying criteria to the evaluation of outcomes and not alternatives makes it possible to remember that we might like O_A a great deal even if, because we lacked sufficient confidence that A would actually lead to O_A, we decided not to choose alternative A after all. With that judgment on the table, it would be possible to look for other alternatives with a greater likelihood of producing O_A.

Criteria selection builds on problem definition—and continues

Of course, the most important criterion is that the projected outcome "solves the policy problem" to an acceptable degree. But this is only the beginning. After all, any course of action is likely to impact the world in many ways, some desired and some not. Each of those impacts—or projected "outcomes," to return to our Eight-Step Path language—requires a judgment on our part of whether and why it is thought desirable. And it is our set of criteria that embodies such judgments. Because any significant impact cries out for such a judgment to be made, the greater the variety of significant impacts the richer the set of criteria we will need to deal with them.

Evaluative criteria commonly used in policy analysis

EFFICIENCY. Maximize individuals' welfare as construed by the citizens themselves. In economic terms, "maximize the sum of individual utilities," or "maximize net benefits." This is the characteristic approach in "cost-effectiveness" and "cost-benefit" analysis. You can call it the "efficiency" criterion.

Note that although "efficiency" has an antiseptic, technocratic, and elitist ring to it, the insistence here that "utility" is to be accounted according to individual citizens' understanding of their own welfare is thoroughly "democratic."

Although "cost-effectiveness" analysis (CE) and "benefit-cost" analysis (BC) sound alike and are frequent traveling companions, they are not the same, and their uses can be quite different. True, both conceptualize a domain of benefits accruing to individual citizens valued (by the citizens themselves) in terms of their "utility." And both view the policy problem as involving some production relationship between resources and beneficial outcomes. However, CE takes one or the other of these (either resources or outcomes) as "fixed" or "targeted"; the analysis then tries to find the best means to manipulate the other one (either maximizing the benefits given the level of assumed resources or else minimizing the amount of resources given the targeted outcome requirement). BC, on the other hand, allows both resources and outcomes to be treated as variable in scale. It is therefore more complicated than CE; for, while both BC and CE concern themselves with the productive efficiency of the program or project, BC is additionally concerned with its scale.

CE analysis is much more common than BC analysis. Indeed, a surprisingly large number of policy issues can be simplified and stylized as CE problems, even though on the surface they may not appear to be likely candidates at all for this sort of treatment. Examples:

— The Mudville Mayor wishes to respond to business complaints that building permits "take forever" to obtain. The CE framework might suggest: minimize delay arising from purely procedural and bureaucratic sources, given that you can spend no more than $500 and are permitted to change only the work-flow in the City Planning office, but not personnel assignments.

— Quake City must upgrade the seismic safety of several thousand buildings constructed of unreinforced masonry. You have a twenty-year time span and no immediate budget constraint, but you wish to accomplish the job with minimum disruption to the lives (and incomes) of the residents and small businesses that may be temporarily displaced by the building renovation process.

Equality, equity, fairness, "justice." There are, of course, a great many different, and often opposed, ideas about what these terms do, or should, mean. Not only ought you yourself to think hard about these ideas, but sometimes you should also take your audience through some of that thinking.

— In California, drivers who do not carry liability insurance leave persons whom they injure in auto accidents at risk of being under-compensated. Many of those who "go bare" are relatively poor. Many other drivers purchase their own insurance against exactly this risk ("Uninsured Motorist" coverage). A policy proposal to pay for all drivers' liability insurance out of a fund created by surcharges at the fuel pump was denounced by some observers as "inequitable" to the poor who currently "go bare." Other observers said that those who "go bare" impose "inequitable" premium expenses or risks of under-compensation on the rest of society, including many individuals who are themselves poor or not very well off. Clearly the analyst needs to include a discussion of the idea of "equity."

— The current debate over whether to retain affirmative action preferences in university admissions for

African-Americans and certain other minorities is sometimes said to pit "fairness" to individuals against "justice" to social groups. This is odd, though, since some philosophers, and most ordinary folk too, suppose that no system claiming to be "just" could contain any features deemed "unfair." Again, the analyst has a job to do in sorting out ideas and language.

Freedom, community, and other ideas. To stimulate thought, here is a (far from complete) list with more ideas about evaluative criteria of possible relevance: free markets, economic freedom, capitalism, "freedom from government control," equality of opportunity, equality of result, free speech, religious freedom, privacy, safety (especially from chemicals, various environmental hazards, etc.), neighborliness, community, sense of belonging, order, security, absence of fear, traditional family structure, egalitarian family structure, empowerment of workers, maintenance of a viable non-profit sector, voluntaryism.

Weighting conflicting evaluative criteria

As we saw in the case of *defining the problem,* when values are at issue, as they are in regard to criterion selection, too, we must reckon how to weight opposing values. There are two general approaches to this problem.

THE POLITICAL PROCESS TAKES CARE OF IT. One approach is simply to allow existing governmental and political processes to make the weighting. Typically this approach will accord primacy to the analyst's employer or client, with derivative influence exercised by those parties in the relevant arena who are in turn important to the employer or client.

THE ANALYST IMPOSES A SOLUTION. A second approach is for the analyst himself or herself to modify—though not replace—the weighting accorded by the employer or client by reference to some overarching philosophical and political conception. The justifications usually offered for this approach are that certain interests, and perhaps philosophies, are typically underrepresented in government and politics, and that the analyst is in a better position than most other participants in the process to "see" or "understand" or "appreciate" this problem of underrepresentation, and is duty-bound, or at least permitted, in the name of fairness and democracy, to right the balance.

For instance, some would argue that, were it not for analysts, efficiency-related criteria would rarely be included and that analysts should, in effect, speak up for the taxpayers whose interests would be squeezed out by better organized advocacy groups. A related argument is sometimes made that certain conceptions of "equity"—in particular the idea that "the beneficiaries of publicly provided goods or services should pay for them"—are underrepresented except among policy analysts. (This conception of equity normally excludes public expenditures deliberately intended to redistribute wealth among citizens.) Other interests that people sometimes claim are underrepresented and therefore need representation by analysts are: future generations, children, people who live outside the jurisdiction making the decisions, ethnic and racial minorities, women, the poor, consumers, animals and plants (ecological entities).

A variant of this approach introduces the idea of an "educational process." Depending on circumstances, the analyst might encourage influential political parties—perhaps including the analyst's boss or principal client—to rethink their existing criteria in the light of facts or arguments the analyst could draw to their attention. In this case the analyst is responsible for opening up a dialogue, and perhaps for trying to infuse it with reason and insight, but would then allow the political process to take over.

Practical criteria

Not all criteria that come into play in an analysis are part of the evaluative plot. Some are purely practical and are part of the analytical plot. These have to do with what happens to an alternative as it moves through the policy and implementation processes. The main ones are: legality, political feasibility, robustness under conditions of administrative implementation, and improvability.

LEGALITY. A feasible policy must not violate constitutional, statutory, or common law rights. However, remember that legal rights are constantly changing and are often ambiguous. It is sometimes worth taking a gamble on a policy that might—or might not—be adjudged illegal when tested in court. (In such cases, advice of counsel to help craft the policy so that its survival chances are enhanced is clearly in order.)

Note, however, that rights alleged to be "natural" or "human" are conceptually quite different from legal rights, despite the semantic similarity. Examples are "abortion rights" or "right to life" or "a woman's right to her own body." Alleged "natural" or "human" rights are sometimes controversial in that some people would like to have them recognized as rights while others would oppose such recognition.

POLITICAL ACCEPTABILITY. A feasible policy must be politically acceptable, or at least not unacceptable. Political unacceptability is a combination of two things:

"too much" opposition (which may be wide or intense or both) and/or "too little" support (which may be insufficiently broad or insufficiently intense or both).

However, do not take a static view of "unacceptability." Always ask yourself the question, "If my favorite policy solution doesn't look feasible under current conditions, what would it take to change those conditions?" You might discover that creative political strategizing can open up options that hadn't been seriously considered before.

ROBUSTNESS. Policy ideas that sound great in theory often fail under conditions of actual field implementation. The implementation process has a life of its own. It is acted out through large and inflexible administrative systems and is distorted by bureaucratic interests. Policies that emerge in practice therefore can diverge, even substantially, from policies as designed and adopted. A policy alternative, therefore, should be robust enough so that even if the implementation process does not go very smoothly the policy outcomes will still prove to be satisfactory.

Some adverse implementation outcomes usually worth worrying about include: long delays, "capture" of program or policy benefits by a relatively "undeserving" and unintended constituency, excessive budgetary or administrative costs, scandal from fraud, waste, and abuse that undermines political support and embarrasses supporters, administrative complexities that leave citizens (and program managers) uncertain as to what benefits are available or what regulations must be complied with.

IMPROVABILITY. Even the best policy planners cannot get all the details right at the design stage. They should therefore allow room for policy implementers to improve on the original design. The most common vehicle for such improvement is participation in the implementation process of individuals and groups whose expertise or point of view had not been included in the design phase.

However, note that the openness which makes for improvability can also, by opening the door to hostile political interests, diminish robustness. Hence, a very careful evaluation of the current factual situation—personalities, institutional demands and incentives, political vulnerabilities, etc.—is usually in order.

(A note on "outcome" and "process." I said above that criteria apply to outcomes and not to alternatives. However, this needs a slight amendment in the case of practical criteria. These criteria do not apply to outcomes but to the prospects an alternative faces as it goes through the policy adoption and implementation process.)

Criteria in optimization models

Up to this point, I have focussed on substantive criteria. A complementary approach is to focus on criteria as understood in a formal sense. In particular, it is helpful to focus initially on one primary criterion, a principal objective to be maximized (or minimized). Typically this principal objective will be the obverse side of your problem definition. For instance, if your problem is "too many homeless families," then your principal objective would probably be "minimize the number of homeless families." If the problem is "the greenhouse effect is growing too rapidly," a good statement of a principal objective might be "minimize growth of the greenhouse effect." Naturally, there are other criteria whereby to judge outcomes, such as costliness, political acceptability, economic justice, etc. These should all enter into the final evaluation. However, it is very likely that unless you focus—initially, at least—on a single primary criterion, and array others around it, you will find yourself getting very confused. As you get deeper into the analysis, and feel more comfortable with a multiplicity of important objectives, you may wish to drop your emphasis on a primary criterion and work on a more complex "objective function."

LINEAR PROGRAMMING. A mathematical (and now computer-accessible) technique for optimizing choice when you have a principal objective or an objective function and a scarce stock of resources for maximizing it is called "linear programming."[1] Often, at least some of the resources—e.g., the agency budget and the available physical facilities promised by a nonprofit agency—are constrained. Even if the problem is not subject to simple quantitative assessment, analysts often find it useful to take advantage of the logical structure of linear programming to conceptualize their task. The conventional formulation then sounds like this: maximize this objective (or objective function) subject to such-and-such resource constraints.

A close relative of the linear programming approach is to think about criteria as falling into three categories: one objective (or objective function) to be maximized; certain constraints; and certain criteria for which, generally, more is better.

— An example from the homelessness problem: "Maximize the number of homeless individuals housed on any given night; subject to the constraints of $50,000 per night total budgetary cost to agency X and to not putting shelters into neighborhoods A and B for political reasons; and trying to give 'more' choice to the beneficiary population as to where they will take shelter..."

----

1. See Stokey and Zeckhauser, ch. 11.

V. Project the Outcomes

Now, for each of the alternatives on your current list, project all the outcomes (or impacts) that you or other interested parties might reasonably care about.

This is the hardest step in the Eight-Step Path. Even veteran policy analysts do not usually do it very well. Not surprisingly, analysts often duck it entirely, disguising their omission by a variety of subterfuges. Hence, the most important advice about this step is simple: Do It.

There are (at least) three great practical as well as psychological difficulties. First, "policy" is about the future, not about the past or the present; but we can never really be certain about how the future will unfold, not even if we engage it with the best of intentions and the most thoughtful of policy designs. Second, "Project the outcomes" is another way of saying, "Be realistic." Yet, realism is often uncomfortable. Most people prefer optimism. "Policy" can actually affect people's lives, fortunes, and sacred honor, for better or for worse. "Making policy," therefore, imposes a moral burden that is heavier than many people care to acknowledge. Understandably, we would rather believe that our preferred or recommended policy alternative will actually accomplish what we hope and that it will impose fewer costs than we might realistically fear. Finally, we come back to what is sometimes called "the 51-49 principle." That is, in the thick of the policy fray, we are driven out of pure self-defense to treat 51% confidence in our projection as though it deserved 100% confidence, with the result that we sometimes mislead not only others but ourselves as well.

The first difficulty, namely that we can never have wholly convincing evidence about the future, compounds the second and third, inasmuch as our wishful thinking is not readily disciplined by reference to empirical demonstrations and proofs. Of course, evidence of some sort is relevant to making projections. But it can come only from experience with similar or analogous policies (see above, *Assemble some evidence.*)

p.16

These cautionary notes notwithstanding, remember that we do not wish to swing towards pessimism either. Realistic projection is our goal.

Causal modeling

p.8

Projection depends on understanding cause-and-effect relations. What relations? First, as I said above under *Define the problem,* the structure of incentives, constraints, and capabilities that hold the policy problem(s) in place; and secondly, the incentives, constraints, and capabilities that might come into play as we would begin to implement a policy.

It is almost always helpful to have a model of the causal structure. Simplify if necessary by breaking your original statement of the problem into separate problems and modeling each one separately. (Remember that your original problem definition was supposed to be only provisional.) A model is usually relatively simple and stylized compared to the complexity and mess of the real world. Some commonly used models:

— A "market" where disaggregated suppliers exchange goods or services with disaggregated demanders. Note that market models can apply to unpriced goods and services. The main idea behind the market model is really "equilibration through exchange." Hence, the market model can be applied to many phenomena other than the production and allocation of textbook goods like widgets or apples.

For instance, you might try to understand the flow of patients into a state mental hospital system in terms of "supply and demand": there is a short-run "supply" of available beds in state hospitals and a per-diem charge for each, while there is a complex "demand" for their use generated by police departments, county psychiatric emergency units, judges, members of the public, etc.

— Production models. Unfortunately, there is not much of an academic literature about the operating logics of the common types of production systems found in public policy, e.g., command-and-control regulation, the provision of information, and all those other "Things Governments Do" briefly described in Appendix B.[1] In any case, the main concern in understanding production systems should be to identify the parameters whose values, when they move out of a certain range, lead most powerfully to breakdown, fraud and abuse, egregious diseconomies, and the distortion of intended purpose. It is also helpful to know about those parameters that matter most when we try to upgrade a production system from mere adequacy to performance levels we might think of as "excellent."

p.69

— Another way to look at production models is through optimization lenses. Operations research models, e.g., queuing, inventory management, Markov processes, are relevant here.[2]

---

1. However, see the chapter on "generic policies" in Weimer and Vining. Also see Lester Salamon, ed., *Beyond Privatization: The Tools of Government Action*, Washington, D.C.: Urban Institute Press, 1989.

— Evolutionary processes: random variation, selection, retention. Usually the selection mechanism is the key to understanding such processes. For example, some regulatory agencies have their caseloads determined largely by complaints. To understand why their enforcement priorities look as they do, you have to understand how actual complainants "select themselves" from among the population of all potential complainants and how agencies give selective attention to certain types of complaints rather than others.

— Organizational and political models.[3]

— The applied social science literature, which is to be found in hundreds of professional journals and uncountable professional research reports, is an extremely rich source of insight and knowledge. No policy analysis should proceed for very long without a systematic review of the literature or consultation with experts who are familiar with the insights and knowledge in the relevant literature.[4]

Attach magnitude estimates

Projecting outcomes often requires you to think not just about the general direction of an outcome but about the magnitude as well. Typically it's not enough to say, "We expect this program to have a very positive effect on reducing unwanted teenage pregnancies."

2. Also see the models, particularly that of case management, in Stephen R. Rosenthal, *Managing Government Operations*, Boston: Little Brown, 1982.

3. For example, those described in Graham Allison's *Essence of Decision* and in Weimer and Vining, chs. 4 and 5.

4. For other ideas, and an excellent discussion of the uses of models generally, see Charles A. Lave and James G. March, *An Introduction to Models in the Social Sciences*, New York: Harper and Row, 1975.

Instead, you'd want to say, "We expect this program to reduce by 100-to-300 the number of unwanted teenage pregnancies per year in this community over the next five years."

Sometimes a "point estimate" of your single best guess about some magnitude will suffice. But in some cases you should provide a range. A convenient way to handle uncertainty in estimation is to answer the break-even question, which is something like this: "What is the minimum level of effectiveness this alternative would have to achieve in order to justify our choosing it?" Of course it comes with these follow-up questions: "And what do we have to believe about how the world works in order to persuade ourselves that we will actually reach that level? ...And do we believe it?" (Also see below, *Confront the Tradeoffs*.)

p.49

The optimism problem

Scenario writing. To counter-bias against natural optimism, systematically review possible adverse scenarios.

Why might the proposal fail to produce the desired outcome, e.g., solving or sufficiently mitigating the policy problem(s)? Insufficient robustness in the implementation process is not only one of the most common problems, but it is frequently a killer. Some horrifying scenarios:

— In a health or safety regulatory program, the scientific or technical knowledge necessary to produce rational and legally defensible standards will prove to be lacking. As a result, five years from now, symbolic politics, corruption, industry capture, or excessive regulatory zeal will have filled the vacuum.

— Time passes, and budgetary resources and political support that had once been available will have slipped away under the impact of electoral change and changes in the economy. The program, begun under nurturing leaders and accompanied by editorialists' applause, becomes consolidated with another program, taken over by a different bureaucratic unit, and eventually disappears.

— A successful state program designed to furnish technical assistance to extremely poor rural counties will have added a mandate to aid many not-so-poor urban counties, with the result that scarce program resources will have been dissipated and squandered.[5]

— A program to subsidize research and development of "fish protein concentrate," intended as a cheap and nutritious food additive, is launched with great fanfare. Five years from now it will prove to have been stalled, permanently, by the Food and Drug Administration not being able to assimilate this product into its standard operating procedures for regulatory review.

Notice that these scenarios are written in the future perfect tense. This proves to be a helpful way to stimulate your imagination.[6]

It often helps your "future perfect thinking" to start with a list of adverse implementation outcomes and to conjure up one or more scenarios about how each of these might have occurred. Remember the list above of such outcomes: long delays; "capture" of program or policy benefits by a relatively "undeserving" and unin-

---

5. I call this scenario "piling on." See Eugene Bardach, *The Implementation Game: What Happens after a Bill Becomes a Law*. Cambridge, MA: MIT Press, 1977.

6. For more details see Karl Weick, *The Social Psychology of Organizing*, Random House, 1979, pp. 195-200.

tended constituency; excessive budgetary or administrative costs; scandal from fraud, waste, and abuse
that undermines political support and embarrasses
supporters; administrative complexities that leave citizens (and program managers) uncertain as to what
benefits are available or what regulations must be complied with.

THE OTHER-GUY'S-SHOES HEURISTIC. Imagine yourself
in the other person's shoes. Say to yourself: "If I were
X, how would I act?" And then proceed to crawl into X's
mind, and play out, in your own mind, what X might
do. Do this systematically for each of the important
stakeholders or other affected parties. The value of
doing this is that you will discover them to be adapting
in surprising ways to the new policy situation you
might be creating, and with results that might cause
trouble for your policy design.

For example, under chemical right-to-know laws,
workers have the right to know what substances they
have been exposed to, and they may examine health
records maintained by employers. If you were a worker,
how might you use this law? Might you use the information to quit your present job? Demand a higher
wage? Demand protective equipment? Sue your
employer? Put pressure on your union representatives?

And how would your union representative react to
such pressure? Might this pressure make the representative's job harder—or perhaps easier in some way?

Now, suppose you were an employer. Given what
you expect your workers might do, you would face
incentives to make adaptations or counter-moves.
Might you stop keeping all health records not explicitly
required by law? Might you continue keeping records
but permit doctors to perform only selected lab tests?

And if you were a worker and saw your employer doing these things, what counter-moves would you make?

Here is another example. At some point in the 1970's the Federal Trade Commission attacked the problem of retailers evading implied warranty obligations for defective products by selling installment debts to banks and other collectors who had no duty, under the so-called "holder-in-due-course" doctrine, to fix the product or to refrain from collecting on the installment debt. The FTC solution was, in effect, to abolish the protections of the holder-in-due-course doctrine. Banks complained that they did not want to go into the toaster repair business. But if you put yourself in the shoes of a bank manager suddenly obliged to become a toaster repairer, might you not have thought of contracting out your repair obligations to repair specialists, or perhaps arranging not to buy installment debts from retailers whom you believed could not be relied upon to make good on their implied warranties, etc.?

UNDESIRABLE SIDE-EFFECTS. Analysts are often cautioned to think about "unanticipated consequences." But this term is not appropriate, for it is often used to refer to perfectly anticipatable, though undesirable, side-effects. Here are some common undesirable but anticipatable side-effects in public programs:

— "Moral hazard" increases. That is, your policy has the effect of insulating people from the consequences of their actions. For example, increasing the size of unemployment benefits has the side-effect of blunting the incentives to search for a replacement job.

— "Overregulation" in the health and safety areas. One possible adverse result, for instance of setting health or safety standards "too high" and enforcing them "too uniformly" is that you increase private sector costs beyond some desirable optimum. For instance, given most people's private preferences for safety, imposing auto bumper standards that cost some $25 per vehicle but which have only trivial effects on improving vehicle crashworthiness would not pass a conventional benefit-cost test. A second adverse result might be that you inadvertently cause a shift away from the regulated activity into some other activity that—perversely—is less safe or less healthful. For instance, some observers argue that overregulating the safety features of nuclear power production has caused a shift towards coal, which, they argue, is much more hazardous than nuclear.

— "Rent-seekers"—that is, interests looking out for profitable niches protected from full competition—distort the program to their own interests. It is not inevitable that suppliers of goods and services to the government, including civil servants, find ways to capture "rents." But it often happens, e.g., with many defense contractors. Rent-seeking also occurs in less obvious ways, e.g., when some regulated firms successfully lobby for regulations that impose much higher compliance costs on their competitors than on themselves.

THE ETHICAL COSTS OF OPTIMISM. It is hard to overstate the importance of worrying about the possible adverse side-effects of otherwise "good" policies, not to mention the possibility that even intended "good" main effects may fail to materialize under many circumstances.[7] The ethical policy analyst always poses the question, "If people actually were to follow my advice, what might be the costs of my having been wrong, and who would have to bear them?" And keep in mind that

---

7. See the Behn and Vaupel chapter on "Assessing Your Ignorance."

the analyst typically is not one of the parties who has to bear the costs of his or her mistakes.

The outcomes matrix

This step in the Eight-Step Path leads you into a dense thicket of information. You will not want to present or discuss all of it in your final report. But at any point along the way you might need to be able to stand back and assess complex and uncertain scenarios for up to eight or ten basic alternatives combined with their principal variants. A convenient way to take in the highlights of all this information is to display it in an outcomes matrix. A smaller version of such a matrix might also prove useful in your final report.

The typical matrix format arrays your policy alternatives down the rows and your evaluative criteria across the columns. Any cell, then, contains the projected outcome of the row alternative as assessed by reference to the column criterion. Here is an example I created in order to compare projected outcomes for three alternative systems to periodically inspect California's ten million automobiles for smog control compliance. In this example, Baker, Smith, and Jones, analysts working for three different government agencies and with somewhat opposed policy views, are making rather different projections of outcomes for each of these alternatives. I record their rival projections in the cells for which they differed.

The Smog Check system involves biennial inspection at the time of vehicle reregistration in any one of several thousand approved service stations. "IM 240" would require biennial inspection using more sophisticated testing machinery at any one of many fewer centralized and specialized testing facilities. "Remote sensing" is an emerging technology that would simply

Table 1: Outcomes Projected by Three Different Analysts for Three Alternative Fleet Inspection Systems

Alternative	How close to needed cleanup	Minimize cost/ ton of pollution reduced ($)	Reduce consumer time (min.)	Reduce test cost to vehicle owner ($)
		Criteria		
IM 240	Baker: 100% Smith: 0%	Baker: <SC* Smith: Millions	Jones: 60 Smith: >60	Jones: <SC* Baker: >SC*
Modified "SC"*	Baker: 50% Smith: 0%	Baker: 1000s Smith: Millions	Jones: 75 Smith: 75	Smith: 35
Remote Sensing	Baker: 0% Smith: 100%	Baker: Millions Smith: 200	Consensus: 0 for most drivers	Consensus: 0 for most owners

* "SC" stands for Smog Check

monitor cars from roadside vans and initiate enforcement measures against those determined to be out of compliance.[8]

If you cannot fill in the cell with a quantitatively expressed description of the projected outcome, you might settle for a verbal descriptor like "very good" or a symbolic descriptor like "+" or "-".

A common error that occurs in labeling the "criterion" columns in such a matrix is to fail to indicate what value is at stake and in what dimensions the measurement is being done. For instance, if you are assessing a rental subsidy program, and you enter a "+" in a column labeled "Landlord/tenant relations," the reader may not know whether you think relations will become more harmonious, more confrontational, less dominated by landlords, less dominated by tenants, or something else. It is not sufficient that your surrounding text might make your intention clear; the matrix labeling itself must be informative. In my illustrative table, I did not simply write "Cleanup" or "Cost" or "Time." Within the space constraints I tried to indicate the metric and the desired direction in which it should move.

Not every criterion will be relevant to every alternative. If that is so, the entry in some of your cells would be "n.a." for "not applicable."

You can simplify the mass of information you need to display and assimilate in your outcome matrix or in any other form, if you eliminate information about outcomes which will be the same for all the alternatives. This is particularly useful if the outcomes they will pro-

---

8. For other examples, see Tables 9-4, 9-5, 9-8, and 9-9 in Stokey and Zeckhauser. See also the discussion in Weimer and Vining, pp. 204-206 and their sample matrix on p. 207.

The Eight-Step Path

duce in common are ambiguous or uncertain: you will be spared the trouble of having to make these difficult projections.

VI. Confront the Tradeoffs

It sometimes happens that one of the policy alternatives under consideration is thought to produce a better outcome with regard to every single evaluative criterion than any of the other alternatives. In that case there are no tradeoffs among the alternatives. This is called "dominance." Usually, though, you are less fortunate, and your job must be to clarify the tradeoffs between outcomes associated with different policy options for the sake of your client and/or audience.

The most common tradeoff is between money and a good or service received by some proportion of the citizenry, e.g., extending library hours from 8 p.m. till 10 p.m. weighed against a cost of $200,000 annually. Another common tradeoff, especially in regulatory policies, involves weighing privately borne costs, such as a company's installing pollution abatement equipment, against social benefits such as improved health and the protection of forests.

As economics teaches us, tradeoffs occur at the margin. Tradeoff analysis tells us something like this: "If we spend an extra X dollars for an additional unit of service Y, we can get an extra Z units of good outcome." This puts the decision maker in the position to answer the question: Does society (or do you) value Z more or less than X? and to then follow the obvious implication of the answer (if yes, decide for another Y; if no, don't).

Some units of service Y can be purchased only in "lumps" larger than one—sometimes much larger. Consider transportation services provided by highways and bridges. Y might be one passenger-trip from A to B, but most transportation construction projects (highway enlargements, new bridge crossings) can be undertaken only for minimum bundles of Y that run into the thousands.

Another example: Suppose the police chief must choose one of two "lumpy" alternatives, $1 million per year for more overtime on the night shift or $250,000 (annualized) for more rapid replacement of police cars. The first alternative is lumpy because the police union insists on a minimum overtime rate for all 150 officers on the shift, and the second is lumpy because the auto supplier charges much less per vehicle after some threshold number of vehicles. If the projected decrease in burglaries, say, from increased overtime were 200 per year and that from newer vehicles were 50, the tradeoff confronting the decision maker at the margin is $5,000 per burglary prevented. In this case "the margin" is a lumpy 150 burglaries and $750,000. (Criteria other than burglary-prevention and cost-efficiency would, of course, be relevant to this problem.)

The multi-attribute problem

Sorting out the tradeoffs is complicated by what is often called "the multi-attribute problem," or the fact that no solution is dominant while the rankings of the several options on the evaluative criteria are not easily commensurable (e.g., by translating them all into dollar values.[1]

---

1. See Stokey and Zeckhauser, pp. 117-133. Their advice on how to deal with the multi-attribute problem is excellent: eliminate clutter by discarding dominated alternatives, and use the method of "computing equivalent alternatives." These methods have their limitations, but they are usually better than less systematic approaches.

Break-even or "switchpoint" analysis

As usual, expressing tradeoffs in terms of magnitude as well as direction is very desirable though not always possible. The difficulty is especially salient when "Z units of good outcome" can't easily be measured in dollars or, more generally, when costs and benefits are not commensurable. In such cases, you can usually be helped by a "break-even" analysis which helps you frame the tradeoff indirectly in some sensible metric. The majority of all policy analyses will require you to perform some sort of break-even analysis.

Many policy proposals, for example, implicitly trade off dollars against risks to life. It might be supposed that in order to assess these proposals you would have to "decide what a human life is really worth"—a task many of us, quite understandably, are unwilling to perform. The task is made somewhat more tractable, however, if you work with quantitative estimates and apply break-even analysis. Suppose, for instance, you are considering whether or not to impose a new auto design standard on the industry that will improve safety and save an estimated 25 lives per year every year into the indefinite future. The cost of meeting the standard is estimated at $50 million every year indefinitely. The tradeoff at the margin appears to be, therefore, "2 million dollars per life." But you don't have to answer the question, "What's a human life really worth?" in order to make at least some sense of this decision. You do have to answer the question, "Is a statistical life (that is, the life of an unknown individual 'drawn' in a random manner from some population, rather than an individualized and named person's life) worth at least $2 million?" That is a break-even analysis sort of question. For reasons best known to yourself, it may be obvious to you that it surely is—or isn't. And, while it's very difficult to decide whether the worth of a statistical life falls on one or the other side of some monetary boundary, it's a lot less difficult than coming up with a point value.

Even this sort of trade-off calculation is troubling to many people, and some find it "morally repugnant." Unfortunately, repugnant or not, it is in a sense inevitable. Whatever position you take on the auto safety design standard described above, you are by implication also taking a position on the dollars/risk-to-life tradeoff: if you favor the standard, you implicitly believe the tradeoff is worthwhile, whereas if you oppose it, you don't. Fortunately, this logical implication has its uses. You may in many circumstances quite sensibly prefer to rely on your "intuition" rather than some complicated systematic method. Once you have reached your conclusion based on intuition, though, you can check your intuition by asking your-self, "Since the implication of my policy choice is that I value X as being worth at least (or at most) thus-and-such, do I really believe that?"

UNCERTAINTY. Another useful application of break-even, or "switchpoint," analysis concerns uncertainties about the future. Sometimes the "bottom line" of an analysis is not a recommendation or a set of value tradeoffs but a well-framed gamble for which a decision-maker must make a choice. Some typical applications:

— Policy X for building a string of four halfway houses for non-violent juvenile offenders looks like it strongly dominates all other policy alternatives provided it really works as planned. But it might not, because: federal grant-in-aid resources might not be forthcoming, or the Mayor might give it lower priority than she now promises, or the halfway houses' neighbors might find a way to block it. You interview your client, a state juvenile justice agency director, and determine that she likes the program so much that she is willing to go for it if it has at least a 50-50 chance of working out. Your analysis can then focus her attention on why, after considerable research, you have concluded that it has a "somewhat better" (or "somewhat worse") chance than 50-50, even though you would find it impossible to specify exactly how much better (or worse).

— Building a new stadium for the Hometown Heroes looks like a good idea, given the nature of the costs and benefits, if average daily attendance turns out to be no less than X thousand. That's the break-even attendance figure for you and the relevant decision-makers. Then it's up to them to decide (a) how confident they are that this break-even level will be reached and (b) whether that degree of confidence is enough to warrant making an affirmative decision. You would then organize your presentation of facts and opinions so that they could focus on these two key issues.

Without projecting outcomes, there's nothing to trade off

A common pitfall in confronting tradeoffs is to think of the tradeoffs as being across alternatives rather than projected outcomes, e.g., "trading off 20 foot-patrolmen in the late night hours against a lower-maintenance-cost fleet of police vehicles." Although there is such a tradeoff, you'll see, with a second's thought, that you can't do anything at all with it. Both alternatives must first be converted into outcomes before genuine tradeoffs can be "confronted." Thus, the competing outcomes might be 50 (plus or minus...) burglaries per year prevented by the patrolmen versus a savings of $300,000 in fleet maintenance.

VII. Decide!

This step appears in the Eight-Step Path as a check on how well you have done your work up to this point. Even though you personally may not be "the decision-maker," you should at this point pretend that you are. Then, decide "what to do" on the basis of your own analysis. If you find this difficult or troublesome, perhaps the reason is that you have not clarified the tradeoffs sufficiently, or that you have not said quite enough about the probability of serious implementation problems emerging (or not emerging), or that a crucial cost estimate is still too fuzzy and uncertain, or that you have not approximated carefully enough the elasticity of some important demand curve, and so on.

Think of it this way: unless you can convince yourself of the plausibility of some course of action, you probably won't be able to convince your client—and rightly so.

Of course, when you *tell your story* to your client or any other audience you might not think it appropriate to include your own recommendation. You might, instead, simply limit your story to a clarification of the relevant tradeoffs and leave the decision completely up to the client.

VIII. Tell Your Story

After many iterations of all the above steps—redefining your problem, reconceptualizing your alternatives, reconsidering your criteria, reassessing your projections, reevaluating the tradeoffs—you are ready to "tell your story" to some audience. The audience might be your client, or it might be broader. It might be hostile, or it might be friendly.

```
┌──────────┐
↓ Iterate │
└──────────┘
```

The New York taxi driver test

Before proceeding further, you need a little "reality check." Suppose you have just caught a cab in New York City. While stalled in traffic, the cabbie asks you about your work. You say you are a "policy analyst working for ..." He says, "What's that?" You explain that you've been working on "the problem of ..." He says, "So, what's the answer?" You have one minute to offer a coherent, down-to-earth explanation before he starts accusing you of being a pointy-headed intellectual or worse. If you feel yourself starting to hem and haw, you haven't really understood your own conclusions at a deep enough level to make sense to others, and probably not to yourself either. Back to the drawing boards until you get it straight.

Now consider the possibility that someone might actually wish to base a real decision or a policy proposal on your analysis. (It's been known to happen.) Even if you, as an analyst, would not have to deal directly with such a tough audience as the New York taxi driver and his kindred, it's not unlikely that someone will have to do so. At the very least, therefore, you'll have to be able to explain your basic story to someone in sufficiently simple and down-to-earth terms that

that "someone" will be able to carry on with the task of public, democratic education.

You, your "client," and your audiences

Assuming you've passed the New York taxi driver test, identify and assess the likely non-taxi-driver audience(s).

First comes your "client," the person or persons whose approval you need most—your hierarchical superior(s), perhaps, or those who are funding your work. What is the relationship between yourself and your client? What you say and how you say it should depend a great deal on whether your relationship is long-term and also on whether it is carried on face-to-face. In particular, how easy will it be for you to correct any misunderstandings that might arise?

Next, think about the larger political environment. Who do you think will "use" the analysis and for what purpose(s)? Will anyone pick up your results for use in an advocacy context? Would you regard this as desir-able? Desirable if certain advocates used your work and undesirable if others did so? Do you want to do anything to "segregate" your policy advice by the type of audience you might want it to reach—or not to reach? Are you, perhaps, inadvertently, using "Smith words" that will alienate certain audiences?

If you are making a clear recommendation, make sure you raise and rebut possible objections to it that various important audiences might think of. Also make sure that you compare it to what you or others might regard as "the next best" course of action, to show why yours is better.

What medium to use?

You can tell your story in written or in oral form. In either case, communicate simply and clearly. The guiding principle is: other things being equal, shorter is always better. Visual aids such as flip charts and over-head transparencies often help in oral presentations. In written presentations, good subheadings and graphics can make reading and comprehension easier.

Your "story" should have a logical narrative flow

The flow should be designed with the reader's (or listener's) needs and interests and abilities in mind. For written presentations, it should be evident to a reader what motivates the entire analysis. This usually implies opening with a statement of the problem your analysis addresses.

Motivating the more detailed steps in the flow of the analysis is also important, that is, the sections, paragraphs, and sentences. Most readers will look for the motivation of any element in the element that immediately precedes it. Therefore, avoid lengthy digressions. On these grounds, be wary of sections you are tempted to label "Background." Similarly, the phrase "Before turning to...," is usually a sign of undigested material. Many readers will be alert to the danger signs; therefore you should be too. The same holds for "It is first necessary to explain/understand the history of..." Policy analysis, remember, is about the future. Perhaps surprisingly, it is often not obvious how, or whether, history affects the future. It might do so, but the burden should be on the writer to show exactly how this comes about.

ONE ALTERNATIVE PER SECTION? A common, though not uniformly applicable, organizing framework is to begin with a good problem definition and then to treat each alternative you consider as a major section. Within each such section you would project the probable outcome(s) of implementing the alternative and assess how likely such outcome(s) might be in the light of some causal model and the associated evidence. Following these discussions you might review and summarize the alternative outcomes and discuss their tradeoffs. (Note that in this framework there is no special discussion of which criteria are to be used. However, sometimes an explicit discussion of this matter is important; it might appear either just before or just after the presentation of the alternatives and their associated outcomes.)

Some common pitfalls

FOLLOWING THE EIGHT-STEP PATH. Sometimes it helps to structure your narrative flow as though you were leading the reader by the hand down the Eight-Step Path. But usually this approach is a mistake. The purpose of the Eight-Step Path, remember, is to help you think through a complicated problem. It is not at all necessary to use it in telling the story, though some aspects of it can sometimes help.

COMPULSIVE QUALIFYING. Don't interrupt the flow of an argument in order to display all the qualifications and uncertainties about some particular element in the argument. A way around this pitfall is to use adjectives or adjective phrases like "most," or "on average," or "more often than not" to state the generality, and then to return to the exceptions in the next section. (Or, if the exceptions and qualifications really can't wait, try a parenthesized sentence or a footnote.)

SHOWING YOUR WORK. Don't include every fact you ever learned in the course of your research. Even if you've done a good and thorough job of research and analysis, most of what you learned will prove to be irrelevant by the time you've finished. That is, you will have succeeded in focussing your attention on "what's really important" and downplaying what only appeared so at the beginning. You don't usually need to take your reader on the same wandering course you were obliged to follow.

LISTING WITHOUT EXPLAINING. Should you list every alternative policy that you intend to analyze in the report before you actually get around to providing the analysis? This is a good thing to do when the alternatives are not numerous, when they are all taken seriously either by you or by your audience, and when the list will prepare the reader's mind for the detailed assessment that will follow. However, if you have many alternatives to consider, the reader will forget what's on the list; and if some of the alternatives turn out to be easily dismissed upon closer scrutiny, you'll simply have been setting up straw men and wasting the reader's mental energy.

Similarly, be cautious about listing every evaluative criterion of interest before coming to the assessment of the alternatives being considered. Usually—though not always—there is not much of interest to be said in a separate section about criteria that can't be better said when you're actually writing the assessment sections.

STYLE. Avoid the pomposity and circumlocutions of the bureaucratic and the academic styles. (Essential reading: George Orwell, *Politics and the English Language*.) Also to be avoided: a "chatty" style, and an "insider's" style, (e.g., "We all understand what creeps our opponents are, don't we?").

A Handbook for Practice

Report format

Unless the report is short, begin with an executive summary.

If the report is over 15-20 pages, say, a table of contents is often helpful. If there are many tables and figures, either in the text or in the appendices, a table of contents for these can be helpful. Detailed technical information or calculations should appear in appendices rather than in the text. However, enough technical information, and reasoning, should appear in the text itself to persuade the reader that you really do know what you're talking about and that your argument is at least credible.

Use headings and subheadings to help keep the reader oriented and to break up large bodies of text; make sure formatting (caps, italics, boldface, indentation) is compatible with, and indeed supports, the logical hierarchy of your argument.

TABLE FORMAT. Current professional practice is very poor with respect to the formatting of tables. Do not imitate it, but strive to improve it. Every table (or figure) should have a number (Table 1, for instance, or Figure 3-A) and a title. The title should be intelligible; it is often useful to have the title describe the main point to be learned from the table, e.g., "Actual Risks of Drinking and Driving Rise Rapidly with Number of Drinks—but Are Greatly Underestimated by College Students." Each row and column in a table must be labeled; and the label should be interpretable without too much difficulty.

Tables normally are either purely descriptive or seek to demonstrate some causal relationship. Regarding the latter, it is usually desirable to create tables that make a single point (or at most two), and that can stand alone without need of much explanation in the text that surround them. It is usually better to use two or three small tables to make two or three points, rather than to use one massive table and then to try to explicate its contents by means of the surrounding text.

Tables usually require footnotes. There should almost always be a "Source:..." line at the bottom of the table. The footnotes sometimes refer to data sources used to make the table, and sometimes attempt to clarify the meaning of the row or column labels, which are necessarily abbreviated.

REFERENCES AND SOURCES. Include page(s) listing references and sources at the end. Books and articles should be cited in academic style (alphabetical order by author). The main point is to provide bibliographic help to curious and/or skeptical readers who want to track down references for themselves. There are several acceptable styles, though a good model is the one used in the book review section of the *Journal of Policy Analysis and Management*, which is simple and direct.

The current trend is toward "scientific citation" in lieu of footnote references in the text. That is, cite last name(s) of author(s) and date of publication in parentheses in text; the reader then checks the references section at the end for the full citation. Sometimes you will want to include a page number in the parenthesized citation as well. If you follow this practice, the references section should list the author(s) and the date before listing the title of the work and publication details.

Legal citation style is quite different. It is sometimes necessary to blend the two. If most of the references are legal, then it is advisable to move all references to bottom-of-page footnotes. However, you can keep the scientific citation format within the footnote.

All footnotes are easier to read if they appear on the same page as the referenced text.

Memo format

[Date]

To: [Recipient name(s), official position(s)]

From: [Your name, position. Sign or initial next to or above your name.]

Subject: [Grammatically correct and brief description of the subject]

[First sentence or two should remind recipient of the fact that she or he asked you for a memo on this subject, and why. Alternatively, you could say why you are submitting this memo on this subject to the recipient at this time.]

[If memo is long, you might open and close with a summary paragraph or two. If you open with a long summary, the closing summary can be short.]

[If memo is long, consider breaking it up with subheads.]

The sound bite and the press release

Most policy analyses do not become the subject of a press release or a radio or TV sound bite. Some do, however; others become candidates for such treatment; and all can profit, even in their extended form, by the analyst's reflecting on how to condense the essential message. Hence, it will probably serve an analytical purpose, and sometimes a political purpose, if you sketch out a press release and/or a few ideas for sound bites. You might also wish to think strategically and defensively to see how an opponent might characterize your work in a press release or sound bite.

Appendix A

Some Generic Opportunities for Social Improvement that Often Go Unnoticed

COMPLEMENTARITY. Two or more activities can be joined so that each might make the other more productive, e.g., public works construction and combatting unemployment.

EXCHANGE. There are unrealized possibilities for exchange that would increase social value. To exploit these, we typically design policies that simulate market-like arrangements, e.g., pollution permit auctions; arrangements to reimburse an agency for services it renders another agency's clients or customers.

UNDERUTILIZED CAPACITY. An example, in many communities, is school facilities that are utilized for relatively limited purposes for only part of the day and for only part of the year—although school officials would be quick to warn that using this capacity without harming school functions is not always easy.

NONTRADITIONAL PARTICIPANTS. Line-level employees of public agencies often have knowledge of potential program improvements that could usefully be incorporated into the agencies' policies and operations. The same is true of the agencies' customers, clients, or the parties whom they regulate.

BYPRODUCTS OF PERSONAL ASPIRATIONS. It is possible to structure new incentives or create new opportunities for personal advantage or satisfaction which can indirectly result in social benefit, e.g., offering to share the benefits of cost-reducing innovations with public sector employees who conceive them and implement them.

DEVELOPMENT. A sequence of activities or operations may have the potential to be arranged so as to take advantage of a developmental process, e.g., assessing welfare clients for employability and vocational interest before, rather than after, sending them out for job search.

RATIONALIZATION. Purely technical rationalization of a system is possible, e.g., shortening queues by deliber-ate spacing of arrival times, or embodying in contracts informal agreements that are vulnerable to decay and misunderstanding.

RUMMAGING. By "rummaging" mentally, one might discover novel uses in seemingly improbable but readily available materials, e.g., using the automobile registration system as a vehicle for carrying out voter registration as well.

MULTIPLE FUNCTIONS. A system can be designed so that one feature can be used to perform two or more functions, e.g., when a tax administrator dramatizes an enforcement case in such a way as both to deter poten-tial violators and reassure non-violators that they are not being made into "suckers" for their honesty.

Appendix B

Things Governments Do

The following list of "things governments do" is meant to stimulate creativity and give you ideas. The way to use it is to think about your policy problem and then go down the list, asking yourself the question, "Might there be any way to use this approach on this problem?"

The "why you might do it" discussion that accompanies each list of "what you might do" is necessarily brief. It is intended principally to be suggestive.

I. Taxes

A. What you might do.

1. Add a new tax

2. Abolish an old tax

3. Change a tax rate

4. Change a tax base

5. Improve collection machinery

6. Tax an externality

B. Why you might do it.

The most common conditions in which "taxes" are a solution are when there is inadequate government revenue for some purpose and—probably more importantly—when the structure of market prices fails to capture the true economic opportunity costs. If market prices are wrong, there are usually deeper structural reasons, like oligopolistic power or government over-regulation of some input, which might bear correcting by other means as well.

Naturally, "too much taxes" can also be a problem. They may be inhibiting useful economic or social activity.

II. Regulation

A. What you might do

1. Add a new regulatory regime or abolish an old one

2. Write new standards or remove old ones

3. Tighten or loosen existing standards

4. Improve the scientific and technical basis for writing standards

5. Close or open loopholes

6. Add, train, or better supervise enforcement personnel

7. Improve targeting of enforcement to catch "bad apples," to increase deterrence, or to increase resource efficiency

8. Raise or lower the level of effective sanctions

9. Tighten or loosen appeals procedures

10. Change reporting and auditing procedures

11. Add, subtract, or improve complaint mechanisms for workers or the public

B. Why you might do it

Distinguish between three quite different types of "regulation." One aims at prices and outputs in "natural monopolies." The Public Utilities Commission regulating local telephone service is an example.

A second type—sometimes called "social regulation"—is common in regard to health and safety issues. It aims to correct imperfections arising from poor market information or from excessive frictions resulting from the use of civil law (usually, tort or contract) remedies. Drug safety regulation by the FDA is an example. This type of regulation is suseptible to two flaws: too little and too much. Scientific uncertainties, technical difficulties of measurement, and political pressures typically lead to both of these problems under varying conditions.

A third type of regulation concerns entry, exit, output, price, and service levels in supposedly oligopolistic industries, e.g., transportation. Administering this type of regulation presents large problems of information collection and of coordinating the outputs of many firms. Politically there are often problems of anti-competitive "capture." The deregulation movement since around 1978 has led to a new appreciation of how much beneficial competition there might be in these industries if government were simply to let go.

Most air and water pollution regulation is thought of as "social regulation." However, administratively (and sometimes politically) it is more like the third type of regulation, inasmuch as the principal laws now on the books involve government agencies in coordinating the outputs of a variety of firms.

III. Subsidies and Grants

A. What you might do

1. Add a new one

2. Abolish an old one

3. Change the level

4. Change the marginal rate

5. Introduce, abolish, or change a formula by which subsidies are allocated

6. Modify the conditions of receipt or eligibility

7. Loosen enforcement

8. Tighten enforcement

B. Why you might do it

Incentive effects: Subsidies and grants are often used to stimulate activities that neither markets nor nonprofit nor voluntary action appear to produce in adequate quantity or quality. They also play an important role in the system of inter-governmental relationships, when one level of government wishes to encourage another level of government to do certain things. They also play a role in the system of relationships between governments and nonprofit organizations.

Wealth effects: Grants and subsidies also transfer resources to people or organizations or levels of government in order to make the recipients wealthier.

Some design problems: It often happens that you want to create incentive effects but not wealth effects, or vice versa. For instance, you might wish to make poor people wealthier via grants and subsidies but without diminishing work incentives. Or you might wish to encourage businesses or universities to undertake more research and development of a certain kind but without unduly enriching them or allowing them to use the subsidies inefficiently.

Note that subsidies and grants are typically administered with various guidelines or conditions attached. The threat to remove a long-time grant or subsidy for violation of the guidelines or conditions can act as a type of regulatory sanction, therefore, making certain grants and subsidies into a peculiar regulatory hybrid.

IV. Agency Budgets

A. What you might do

1. Add a lot to the budget

2. Add just a little to the budget

3. Hold the budget at last year's level

4. Cut the budget a little

5. Cut the budget a lot—to the point of beginning to terminate the agency.

6. Shift allocations from one budget item to another

B. Why you might do it

You might want to adjust an agency's budget according to whether you like what it does. In addition, how you manipulate an agency's budget sends political signals about the degree of satisfaction or dissatisfaction with the agency's performance, and so may be thought to have incentive effects as well as wealth effects. It is not easy to use the budget as a means of creating incentive effects, however.

V. Information

A. What you might do

1. Require disclosure

2. Direct government rating or certification

3. Standardize display or format

4. Simplify information

5. Subsidize production of information

6. Subsidize dissemination of information

B. Why you might do it

Information production, dissemination, and validation may be suboptimal due to the declining average (and sometimes marginal) cost nature of the activity. Information consumption may be suboptimal due to the hidden costs of consumption (such as time spent reading or hearing or interpreting or sifting or verifying).

VI. Modify Structure of Private Rights

A. What you might modify or create

1. Contract rights and duties

2. Property rights

3. Liability duties

4. Family law

5. Constitutional rights

6. Labor law

7. Corporate law

8. Criminal law

9. Dispute-resolving institutions other than litigation and courts

B. Why you might do it

No simple summary can do justice to this question. In recent years, though, two of the biggest issues that have attracted the attention of policy analysts and economists interested in legal institutions concern the economically efficient incidence of risk—it should fall on the party that can manage it at the lowest social cost—and the costs involved in administering any adjudicative system. Since private-law duties and rights do a lot to allocate risk (e.g., if your product exposes the user to risk and ultimately injury, you may be liable for damages, unless perhaps he abused or misused it or agreed to assume the risks of use), adjusting laws is sometimes a powerful policy intervention mechanism. As to the administrative and adjudicative costs, much creative thinking has gone into finding ways to bring these down.

In addition to these "economic" concerns, there is also concern about compensation for harms. Laws can be changed so as to shift wealth—in some prospectively actuarial sense or in a real present-time sense—among different interests or classes of people.

The wealth-shifting and risk-shifting effects of legal changes may both work in the desired direction, or they may work at cross-purposes. In addition both may work together with, or at cross-purposes with, the desire to reduce administrative and adjudicative costs.

VII. Modify Framework of Economic Activity

A. What you might do

1. Encourage competition

2. Encourage concentration

3. Control prices and wages (and profits)

4. Decontrol prices and wages (and profits)

5. Control output levels

6. Decontrol output levels

7. Change tax incentives up or down

8. Provide public jobs

9. Abolish public jobs

B. Why you might do it

Supporting more government intervention: On the supply side, there may be monopoly or oligopoly problems. On the demand side, consumers may be relatively non-mobile or otherwise vulnerable to exploitation—and the same might be true of workers.

Supporting less government intervention: You might decide that political forces had captured the government administrative apparatus and perverted the intent; or you might decide that the information costs to government entailed in doing the job well were simply too high; or you might think that technology had changed and made an older form of government intervention less appropriate or effective or efficient.

VIII. Education and Consultation

A. What you might do

1. Warn of hazards or dangers

2. Raise consciousness through exhortation or inspiration

3. Provide technical assistance

4. Upgrade skills and competencies

5. Change values

6. Professionalize the providers of a service through training or certification or licensing

B. Why you might do it

People may be unaware of a problem or an opportunity. They may be careless or unfeeling. There might be too many untrained or unskilled people in jobs demanding too much responsibility.

IX. Financing and Contracting

A. What you might do

1. Create a new (governmental) market

2. Abolish an existing (governmental) market

3. Alter reimbursement rates

4. Change the basis for reimbursement (e.g., cost-plus, price per unit, sliding scale dependent on quantity, performance bonuses or penalties, etc.)

5. Lease governmentally-held resources

6. Alter the user fee structure

7. Redesign bidding systems

8. Change contract enforcement methods

9. Furnish loans

10. Guarantee loans

11. Subsidize loans

12. Set up a public enterprise

13. Dismantle a public enterprise

14. "Privatize" a hitherto public enterprise

15. Modify insurance arrangements

16. Change procurement practices

B. Why you might do it

Capital and/or insurance markets might be working inefficiently. The governmental contracting and procurement machinery might not be operating well: it might be too rigid, or too corrupt, or too expensive, or too slow.

X. Bureaucratic and Political Reforms

A. What you might do

The number of possibilities is too great to list. It ranges across such activities as reorganizations, replacing top supervisory personnel, improving information systems, raising wages and salaries, etc.

B. Why you might do it

The substantive reasons are too numerous to list. We may note, though, that in many policy contexts there are important political and symbolic consider-ations for undertaking bureaucratic and political reforms. The political considerations often involve enhancing the power of one social interest or point of view at the expense of another. The symbolic consider-ations often involve ducking the really hard or impossi-ble problems at the social level in favor of doing something readily seen in a domain over which govern-ment appears to have control (that is, its own opera-tions).

Part II

Gathering Data
for Policy Research

Gathering Data for Policy Research*

We are recognizing, increasingly, the need for better analysis of public programs and agency performance. The techniques of measurement and the analytical approaches employed in such work are ordinarily drawn from the several social science disciplines, and they improve at about as rapid a rate as theses disciplines manage to improve them for their own use. A great deal has been written about these techniques and approaches by sociologists, psychologists, economists, and political scientists, and the policy researcher should certainly become familiar with these writings. The methods of data collection for policy research, however, are not, and should not be, entirely coincident with those used in the social sciences.[1] On balance, indeed, I believe there is more difference than similarity. In general, it is what I shall call the strategic aspects of policy research that set it apart from social science research, and which constitute the focus of this paper.

* This essay was originally published in *Urban Analysis*, 1974, Vol. 2, pp.117-144 by Gordon and Breach Science Publishers Ltd.

1. In many ways the appropriate techniques are closer to those of high-class journalism than they are to social science research. Unfortunately, there is no literature in the journalism field that systematically describes these techniques in sufficient detail for our purposes. The best textbook treatment of the subject which I have found, however, is Mitchell V. Charnley, *Reporting*, 2nd ed., New York: Holt, Rinehart and Winston, 1966, ch. 7 ("The News Beat"), especially pp. 85-93. A very perceptive and informative account of how journalists actually work is provided in Leon V. Sigal, *Reporters and Officials: The Organization and Politics of Newsmaking*, Lexington, Mass.: D.C. Heath, 1973.)

Introduction

Consider the problem confronting an aspiring young policy researcher preparing an analysis of water pollution control programs in Blue Lake. He knows there is a dirty lake, that there is federal, state, and local legislation directed toward the end of cleaning up the lake (or preventing it from getting much dirtier), and that there is a federal Environmental Protection Administration office in the area that has something to do with administering some or all of the relevant anti-pollution policies or programs. But the researcher needs to know more. He needs to map the present policies and programs, their political environment, the way the bureaucracies function to implement them, and the criteria by which experts and laymen evaluate them. He also needs to make some decisions about how he himself will evaluate them, then to learn what data are relevant to these criteria, and finally to figure out how to obtain these data. If he is planning to recommend changes in existing programs, then he must, in addition, learn what sort of changes the present set of relevant actors might be prepared to make or are capable of making. He must also assess the relative advantages of different types of change strategies, e.g., working quietly from within or applying public pressure from without.

These are large questions, but the researcher's resources in time, energy, money, and the good will of potential informants and interviewers, are probably not at all large. Preferably he would like to finish the study in no more than six months, let us say—and he does not want to waste the first five simply getting his bearings. Where is he to begin? And, once begun, how is he to proceed?

The Eight-Step Path

I. In the beginning

The very first step is simple: start with what you know. This injunction may seem self-evident or trivial or both. In fact, however, it is common for people to act in contradiction with it. Confronted by a new and challenging research task, they expect to flounder anxiously for a few weeks or months. And behold they do; for feeling stupid makes you so. Rarely is this necessary, however. A few facts, or even vague recollections, plus some intelligent reasoning can usually move the project onto firm footing surprisingly quickly. Suppose, for example, you are asked to do a policy analysis of "the future of the Wichahissic bituminous coal industry." a subject as remote from your interest or previous experience as galactic spectroscopy. You might take stock by writing a memo to yourself as follows:

1) I was probably asked to do this study because someone thinks the future of the Wichahissic bituminous coal industry is pretty bleak—or else because it is looking up. If the former, the results will probably be used to justify some sort of government subsidy; if the latter, the results will be used for promotional purposes by the industry itself or by local merchants whose livelihood depends on the health of the industry.

2) The future of any industry depends in part on market demand. The demand for coal has probably been declining, partly due to the availability of substitute fuels.

3) Maybe there are high production costs which imperil the health of the industry. Could it be that coal-mining technology is underdeveloped. If so, why? Perhaps the coal fields are running out and the technology was not developed to handle poor, as opposed to rich, deposits.

A Handbook for Practice

4) There were a lot of miners' strikes a few years ago. Are labor-management relations better or worse now? Are wage demands forcing the companies to go under? Write the United Mine Workers for information.

5) Railroads and coal. Coal transportation depends on railroads—so if the railroads are sick, could coal be well?

6) Ecology and coal. Coal is black and sooty and gives off a lot of smoke. Surely this must be an ecological menace. Who, if anyone, is paying attention to this problem? Or is it really a problem? Coal mining destroys the beauty, and probably the ecology, of the countryside. Is this really so? Might the Sierra Club have useful data on these questions?

7) Perhaps coal is not sick, just bituminous coal. Maybe the anthracite industry is flourishing. Surely there must be a trade association of coal-mining companies with data here—call up the nearest big coal company and find out its name and address from their public relations office.

8) Perhaps coal is okay, but Wichahissic is problematic. But then again, Wichahissic does not seem to be as much in the news as Pokanoka, whose plight seems to be the archetype for "the depressed area." Check BLS (Bureau of Labor Statistics) for unemployment figures here.

Writing memos of this kind to yourself is useful not only at the beginning of the project but whenever you feel yourself beginning to drift towards panic or confusion.

Following this initial stock-taking, the researcher should think of himself as designing, executing, and periodically readjusting a research strategy which will exploit to advantage certain predictable changes in his potential for gaining and utilizing information:

1) LOCATING RELEVANT SOURCES. Over time, the researcher decreases his uncertainty about what is worth knowing and how to learn it.

2) GAINING AND MAINTAINING ACCESS TO SOURCES. (a) Over time, the researcher augments his capacity to obtain interviews from busy or hostile persons, and to obtain data which are not clearly in the public domain. (b) Over time, the researcher also—and unavoidably— uses up his access to certain sources, and he must therefore conserve such an exhaustible resource to be used only when the time is propitious.

3) ACCUMULATING BACKGROUND INFORMATION AS LEVERAGE. Over time, the researcher improves his capacity to interpret data and to force it out of reluctant sources, thereby increasing further his background knowledge.

4) PROTECTING POLITICAL CREDIBILITY. Over time, the research process itself creates an environment which will either help or hinder the adoption and implementation of the researcher's eventual recommendations.

The optimal strategy for managing any of these may conflict with the optimal strategies for dealing with the others. Each of these problems will be discussed in a separate section, with the final section of this paper reserved for a brief treatment of dilemmas arising from trying to meet all strategic imperatives simultaneously. I assume throughout that the reader is an inexperienced policy researcher who has had academic training in the social sciences. Hence I go to some lengths, at various points, to allude to differences between social science research methodology and the methods of policy research.[2] I trust that the more experienced researcher will also find some profit in the arguments of this paper—even if only to conceptualize more clearly what he has already learned to do intuitively.

Another clarification about the intended audience is also in order. The policy researcher starts his task with certain resources and constraints, some of which are derived from his own experience and personality and others from his institutional location. Although institutional location is especially important in designing an optimal research strategy, it will not be discussed in this paper. Suffice it to note that the resources and constraints of a legislative staff assistant are quite different from those of his counterpart in a bureaucratic setting and are even more dissimilar from those of a Nader raider. The strategic advice offered here is intended to be sufficiently general to meet the needs of researchers in any of these circumstances, however.

II. Locating Relevant Sources

Unlike most social science research, most policy research is derivative rather than original. That is, it is produced by creative play with ideas and data already developed by others. Only occasionally does the policy researcher set out to generate his own data or assume

---

2. This paper is also addressed, of course, to policy researchers trained in the natural sciences or in technical fields like operations research or econometrics. My reason for addressing in particular persons with training in the "softer" social sciences is that their methodological traditions are often generalized inappropriately to policy research. Having been trained as an academic social scientist myself, furthermore, I have some personal sense of the difficulties of shedding commitments to traditional, but inappropriate, research methods.

responsibility for inventing *de novo* a bright policy idea. His role is preeminently that of discovering, collating, interpreting, criticizing, and synthesizing ideas and data which others have developed already. To be sure, social science research often works like this too, but it also places a much higher premium on originality. In a sense, the policy researcher becomes an expert on experts, "experts" here being those scholars and men of experience who are thought to be relatively sophisticated about the policy area.[3]

A. Documents and people

In policy research, almost all likely sources of infor-mation, data, and ideas fall into two general classes: documents and people. By "documents" I mean any-thing which has to be read—books, journal articles, newspapers and magazines, government reports, sta-tistical archives, inter-office memoranda, position papers, bulletins, etc. By "people" I mean both individ-uals and groups; and the means of consulting such

---

3. There is of course no point in trying to make airtight distinctions between activities which are in fact similar and are performed by people who think of themselves as being diffusely deserving of any or all professional designations like social scientists, evaluation researcher, applied social scien-tist, policy analyst, or policy researcher. Moreover, I recognize that social science and policy research take many forms. For the purposes of this discussion, however, I have in mind an "ideal type" academic social scientist who, in order to study, say, loan sharking, interviews 75 loan sharks and 50 cus-tomers, and an "ideal type" policy researcher employed by a legislative committee who, for a similar study would sacrifice such precise knowledge for cruder information about a more variegated set of actors and policy options, including the police, businessmen, bankers, state legislators, newspaper-men, and of course some loan sharks and their clients.

personal sources is typically through asking questions and listening for answers. Research on any policy problem should usually entail a canvass of both types of source, though some researchers tend to overemphasize one at the expense of the other. Sometimes this tendency occurs out of habit: if the researcher starts out interviewing experts, experienced administrators, and other informed persons, he continues doing so until he comes to define "interviewing" as what his job is all about. The researcher slowly forgets the fact that the experts themselves typically obtained their expertise from documents, and that much of what administrators offer can be found in agency reports, legislative hearings, published statutes and regulations, and so on. Another reason for getting stuck in one medium and neglecting the other is the personal preference for either passive or active modes of inquiry, that is, for libraries (or files, in an organizational setting) as opposed to field work, or else a preference for less rather than more personal interaction. It is usually desirable not only to consult both types of sources, documents and people, but also to consult them in alternating order: a spate of interviewing followed by a retreat to the library followed by another round of interviewing, etc. If for no other reason, there is probably a psychic economy in arranging and executing a field work agenda in a consolidated time span, as there is in collecting and exploring a large body of documentary material.

In a more general way, however, it should be remembered that one source should be used to locate another and that this branching out can just as easily lead from one medium to the other as it can from source to source of the same type of medium. More explicitly: people lead to documents as well as to other people, and documents lead to people as well as to other documents. There are thus four basic branches on the tree of knowledge, each of which we shall discuss in turn.

1) PEOPLE LEAD TO PEOPLE. Often one informant leads spontaneously to another by remarking during the course of an interview or conversation, "Have you seen X yet—he's very knowledgeable about...?" This information can be stimulated by the researcher himself, by asking questions like, "Who else would be a good person to talk to about...?" This might be more specific: "Who would be a good person to see in Agency Y?" For reasons of tact, one might frame the question more tentatively: "Do you think it would be advisable to talk to...—or do you think that would not be advisable?" Sometimes it is a good idea to ask the informant explicitly if his name can be used in seeking an appointment with the person he has suggested. This gives him an opportunity to protect himself if he does not, and an opportunity to encourage name-dropping if he believes it will serve his interests. (That is, A may wish B to know that A has spoken of him as "a knowledgeable person." or words to that affect.) Make sure that the informant provides a sufficient address or telephone number of anyone he recommends seeing so that it is possible to locate the person.

Knowing whom to stay away from is often an important by-product of inquiries like these. If the informant is trusting and wishes to be helpful, he may volunteer a cautionary aside like, "if you do go see X, you'll probably find him reserved if not unsympathetic." Unless X is a very important step in the developmental sequence at that moment, this might very well be a clue not to approach X until better groundwork has been laid for such a meeting. Another important by-product of such inquiries is a file of information on who is friendly, or antagonistic, to whom. Such information will be useful in constructing a map of political and administrative feasibility for any new program that the researcher might eventually propose.[4]

2) PEOPLE LEAD TO DOCUMENTS. Just as one can ask people whom else to see or talk to, one can also ask them what else to read and how to obtain it. In visiting people in their offices, you can sometimes get useful hints by scanning the bookshelves and the papers on tables and desk tops for titles and authors or agency names. Also take all the documents away from the interview that the informant is willing to give you, even if you are not sure how relevant they are. The chances are good that you will turn up some interesting new material in the collection you eventually develop; and in any case, you may avoid a trip to the library should you later wish to quote them or to report precise bibliographical information. Finally, have yourself put on mailing lists, so as to be on the receiving end of whatever stream of reports, bulletins, newsletters, circulars, etc., are distributed by organizations operating in the policy area.

3) DOCUMENTS LEAD TO DOCUMENTS. Anyone who has ever written a substantial academic research paper in history or the social sciences has probably learned how to use one document to discover another through footnotes and bibliographies. The same procedures work in policy research too. In addition, one frequently uncovers references which are incomplete from a strictly academic point of view, but which are still useful for policy research. These are references to agencies or organizations (and even individuals) that have an ongoing

---

4. See Eugene Bardach, *The Skill Factor in Politics: Repealing the Mental Commitment Laws in California*; Berkeley: University of California Press, 1972; and Arnold Meltsner, "Political Feasibility and Policy Analysis," in *Public Administration Review*, Nov./Dec 1972, pp. 859-867.

The Eight-Step Path

responsibility for, or interest in, the policy area. Some of these can be expected to sponsor studies, reports, position papers, etc., which will prove invaluable to the researcher. It might, of course, require a certain ingenuity to find out their addresses. Fortunately, this is not a problem for most agencies, special study commissions, or task forces that operate under public auspices.

Once research is under way "documents lead to documents" in a relatively straightforward way and without much difficulty. The problem is in knowing where to start when the research effort is just beginning. Ordinarily, the researcher will want an overview of the policy area at this early point; and it is advisable to think of three rather distinct dimensions along which to take sightings: the nature of the social problem; the array of existing public and private responses to the problem; and patterns of political conflict and Cooperation among actors (both collective and individual) making those responses.

As to the first, a scholarly or semi-scholarly book of recent vintage is probably the best place to begin. Indeed, several such books make the best beginning. How should one find them? There are no doubt many ways, but a fairly reliable one involves thinking of an academic discipline or field which is closely related to the policy area; locating the principal scholarly journals published in that field; and then consulting the most recent issues of those journals for book reviews, footnotes, and bibliographies which report book titles of probable interest and significance.

The array of existing policy responses is best approached through identifying the leading public agency operating in the policy areas. From their periodic reports to the legislature, public relations newsletters, and special studies it is usually possible to glean information about a wide variety of other programs and actors in the area. Sometimes these can be usefully supplemented by reports produced on the legislative side by committee staff evaluating ongoing policies or trying to justify new directions.

One cannot go through all the above scholarly and governmental publications without learning something about the pattern of political conflict and cooperation in the policy area; yet this information may still not be sufficient for the initial overview one seeks. Since politics is often a prime concern of newspaper reporters and magazine writers, consult the New York Times index and the principal periodical indexes for story titles which suggest coverage of such topics.

4) DOCUMENTS LEAD TO PEOPLE. Once having read, or read about, the work done by certain experts, academic or otherwise, the researcher might wish to consult with them face-to-face or by telephone. You should be wary, of course, of mistaking the nominal author of a study for the real one, particularly when the former is a person or group in officialdom. The nominal authors of Supreme Court decisions, to take an extreme example, are the Justices; but the real authors are usually their clerks, who in turn probably draw most of their arguments from the briefs filed by the attorneys to the case. Similarly, you should look behind the agency official whose name appears on the cover of a report to the staff who did the work and may be named on the inside pages or referred to in a preface.

Of course, the researcher is not interested in the names of experts alone. The nominal as opposed to the real authors of a study may be important sources of political information. Their nominal credit as authors or study participants probably reflects their political significance (in someone's eyes, at least); and their willingness to accept nominal responsibility for the work perhaps signifies their readiness to play a public relations role of some sort—and perhaps to granting interviews to peripatetic policy researchers.

B. Second-hand information

To find out what Senator A is doing or thinking about a policy problem, one need not necessarily ask the Senator himself. Tens or hundreds of individuals may know the answer, or at least part of the answer. Such second-hand information must be used cautiously, and constantly checked for bias or error. But it is in no *a priori* sense inferior to information obtained first-hand, which has its own biases and factual errors. To use a legal analogy, one relies for "truth" on witnesses rather than on the defendant himself, who after all cannot easily or prudently be asked to testify against himself. Sometimes it makes sense to obtain first-hand information as a supplement to the other, particularly if there is reason to think that failure to do so might ultimately jeopardize the credibility of the final research product.

The use of second-hand sources is especially important in seeking political feasibility data. Suppose, for example, that you are planning to recommend that emergency ambulance services be centralized under the city police department, and you want to estimate the probable reaction of the fire chief to such a recommendation. You could go ask the fire chief himself, but he might not be willing to tell the truth, especially if he were going to hold out his acquiescence in return for better terms or for some side-payment. That is, he might in principle be willing to go along with the change—he might indeed be an enthusiast for it—but for bargaining purposes he might not be prepared to let on. On the other hand, he might really be against it, but not be willing to let on to that either because he thinks people might call him an obstructionist. In either case the fire chief is not an easy source for this information. Eventually it might be desirable to ask him his opinion directly, but one could probably learn as much or more by asking instead a variety of second-hand sources like a veteran city hall reporter, rank-and-file firemen, someone in the city manager's office, and someone from the police department.

C. Multiple sources of first-hand information

Suppose you wish to know about the past relation-ship between the police and the fire departments. Have they been relatively cooperative, antagonistic, or indif-ferent? If for some reason you do not wish to ask the fire chief, it is always possible to ask the police chief since he has been a partner to these relations as much as the fire chief. He may have a different view or inter-pretation of these relationships, but he is as much a participant and his knowledge just as direct.

There are numerous applications of this principle. If the researcher wants to know what happened at a par-ticular meeting to which he was denied admission (or could not go for other reasons), there are many partici-pants to query. If he wants to know how one particular participant behaved at that meeting, he does not nec-essarily have to ask the participant, he can ask others who attended. If the researcher wishes to see a memo-randum sent by Smith to Jones, he can ask either Smith or Jones, depending on which one he believes will be more agreeable—or obtain a photocopy in the hands of a third party.

The notion of systematically using second-hand sources and the notion of multiple-sources for first-hand information is foreign to the spirit and practice of much social science research. Social science research typically assumes that when one wants to know the mental states or the conduct of a given individual, the best source is that individual. It then worries about how to devise measuring instruments and interviews which will register these facts about the individual with the least distortion. Often this is quite appropriate for the questions about which one does basic and original research, when the object is to get pure data for pure understanding. But in policy research the problem is to get a sufficient understanding of the world so as to be able to make estimates about alternative courses of action. Since there is much uncertainty about the future, and so many uncontrollable variables that will enter into future action, too much precision about the past and present is frequently apt to get in the way.

D. The search for sources and the search for knowledge

At the beginning of a policy research project, the researcher faces a dual uncertainty, about what he thinks he ought to know and where he can turn to learn it. These are interdependent, in the sense that the reduction of one type of uncertainty is both a consequence of and a condition for the reduction of the other.

Consider first what happens as the researcher clarifies his ideas about what he thinks he ought to know. Simultaneously, he is able to exclude certain sources he would otherwise have consulted, and because he knows better what his objectives are, he is able to intensify his search for sources of more certain relevance. This is the classic research model, in which ends determine means, that is to say, a constantly evolving set of knowledge objectives gives shape to the strategy of source selection and consultation. It is as applicable to policy research as to any other sort of social inquiry.

Its exact opposite is also applicable—and quite properly so, though many would wish to deny it. Because the cost of searching for adequate sources is so high in terms of time and energy, when one finds a rich source it may be wise to mine it intensively, even if that decision slightly alters one's original knowledge objectives. If you wish to make recommendations to the state legislature concerning the reduction of criminal recidivism rates, for instance, the most relevant data source, recidivism in that particular state, may not be as rich—and therefore useful—as data from the California Bureau of Criminal Statistics, which is unrivalled in the nation as a collector of such data.[5]

One danger in this sort of pragmatism is that you will spend too much of your time on what appears to be a rich source, not knowing that there are much richer ones just around the corner. That is why it is wise to invest a good deal of time initially in canvassing a variety of possible sources and developing a broad overview of both the policy area and what means there are to learn about it. After this initial survey it is possible to return to sources that look unusually rich. This procedure also guards against the second, and more important, danger in letting the sources guide you, that you

---

5. It is clearly beyond the scope of this paper to catalogue the archives and statistical series that might prove especially rich for explorations into all, or even the most common policy areas. A researcher looking into housing problems will quickly learn from his canvas of the academic literature that the United States Bureau of the Census publishes a special housing survey. As I indicated in the opening paragraph of this paper, good policy research does, and should, draw upon the knowledge and techniques of relevant academic disciplines.

The Eight-Step Path

might lose sight of more desirable and feasible knowledge objectives. In the final analysis, there must be a balance between the classic model of ends (knowledge) dictating means (sources) and the pragmatic model of ends evolving out of the means one has at hand.

III. Gaining access and engaging assistance

In policy research, a resource of particular importance is access to informants you wish to interview. If you wish to interview Assemblyman Jones, for example, you must persuade the appointments secretary that you are on serious business and that in any event you will not be put off. You must arrange an appointment for a not-too-distant date, and persist even after Jones breaks the first appointment and fails to show up for the one made in lieu of that one. If you wish to interview Jones subsequent to that first time, you must take pains to keep this possibility open, and perhaps to foster it by your conduct during the first interview.

Often it is necessary to engage the active assistance of certain informants. From the researcher's point of view, engaging such assistance is merely a special case of the problem of gaining access; it is access in a higher degree, so to speak. Such assistance is desirable especially when you are trying to collate and interpret statistical data in the possession of some agency. Often these data are in a "raw" state; that is the data are in the files but need to be collated and tabulated. Sometimes the data are in a semi-processed condition; that is, they have been collated and tabulated, but they have not been put in a format which is intelligible to the researcher. (They are still in a format that is intelligible to the program managers, but this format does not reveal the meaning of the data fully to the researcher.) In such a case, the researcher may wish to know about seeming inconsistencies in the classification of cases, or about the meaning of certain class designations which the managers have developed for their own decision-making. Finally, there are data which are processed for public use but which have not been processed completely or adequately for your purposes. Suppose the intramural evaluation staff of a state penal institution, for example, has issued its annual report on releases and recidivists, but one cannot tell from the report how reliably they have ascertained the prior arrest and conviction record of the so-called "first offenders." Did they rely on probation officer reports? On prison records? Records from other states? As a recent report on federal statistics has put it, the "error structure" of an agency's data is often not known to the agency; and if it is, it might not be made known to the public.[6] In this case, as in the case of raw and semi-processed data, interpretive assistance is needed from the agency itself. How much assistance it is willing to give depends in part at least on how well the researcher has cultivated good working relations with the agency and its personnel.

A. Getting an appointment

Why should any informant grant you, a mere policy researcher, an interview? American manners and mores provide the most compelling reasons; it is part of our definition of courtesy. If someone talks to you, even through your appointment secretary, you are supposed to talk back. Of course, the more powerful, busy, or politically defensive the personage besought, the less force will simple courtesy apply in your favor. In such

---

6. Harry Grubert, "How Much Do Agencies Know About Error Structure?" in Report of the President's Commission on Federal Statistics, *Federal Statistics*, Washington, D.C.: Government Printing Office, 1971, vol. 2, pp. 297-334.

cases, you might try to appeal to a sense of noblesse oblige or, if you have a prestigious institutional affiliation, to a willingness to acknowledge your caste privileges. In addition, many people simply feel flattered by having an outsider—even a policy researcher—wanting to listen to them.

More reliable, however, than these appeals to mere sentiment is an appeal to political self-interest. Try to indicate that the outcome of your research is likely to have a bearing on the interviewee's (or his agency's) political fortunes and ambitions. It would therefore be prudent for him to be cooperative, arrange for you to hear his (or his agency's) point of view, and indeed to use the interview setting to assess the relevant political implications of your work. Of course, it may require some fast talking over the telephone, when you call for an appointment, in order to set his mind thinking in these directions. In dealing with an appointments secretary, who will probably be even less sensitive to your political cues, you might have to make your points indelicately explicit. Instead of relying on the vagaries of a telephone conversation or an appointment secretary, it might be useful to write a letter requesting an interview. In such cases, it is advisable to follow up the letter with a telephone call checking on the status of your request.

Many of the informants whom you will interview are acquainted with each other and will occasionally talk among themselves about you and your work. It is best to have such discussions serve your interests rather than work against them. You should therefore attempt to develop a reputation as a competent, knowledgeable, and energetic researcher who is likely to produce something of intellectual or political significance. The best way to develop such a reputation is actually to be such a person; but in addition, certain stratagems may prove useful. Attempt, for instance, to become "a familiar face," by attending meetings and conferences which your potential informants attend, and by loitering around office cafeterias or after-hours places which they frequent. Try to impress people with your ability to gain entree to meetings which are only quasi-public in nature, and by talking in public places to important personages. Of course, all this familiarity will backfire if you appear pesky or inept, hence some judiciousness is in order. Also you should appear to be learning quickly and critically while in these settings, rather than observing passively and dully. Taking notes fast and furiously is occasionally a good stage prop as well as useful in its own right. So too is animated conversation, preferably observed rather than overheard.

Do not imagine that field work can proceed rapidly or smoothly. For the most part, you are the captive of other people's schedules. You can expect delays of three days to three weeks between the time you request an appointment and the appointment date—and even longer if your informant eventually breaks the appointment and reschedules it for a few weeks later! Sometimes it seems that research is mainly idle waiting. This problem is particularly acute if delay in seeing one informant is a bottleneck to seeing others. To minimize idleness, it is a good idea to have two or three independent streams of interviewing running simultaneously, so that a bottleneck in any single stream cannot halt your work altogether.

B. Cultivating access

Securing repeated access to an individual or agency presents different problems from securing a one-time-only appointment. Courtesy is of almost no use here; the political motive, conversely, is critical. Since the political impact of your work on certain individuals and organizations will almost certainly be adverse, some doors will inevitably be closed to you. Beyond a certain point, there is nothing to be done about them, except to seek alternative means of entry.

A perceived political affinity helps, but by itself it is not sufficient. It is virtually impossible to secure repeated access to people unless they trust and like you. To put it another way, securing repeated access depends in large part on building rapport with the objects of your study. Building rapport takes time, especially if you are not inclined to appear more friendly and congenial than you really feel. Rapport follows most of all from simple exposure. You should think of yourself as an anthropologist who has to spend several months living among the tribe he is studying before being allowed to observe certain sacred rituals and practices.[7] Thus you may find it useful to make repeated visits to the agency, say, either for interviewing or for some other purpose, like document gathering and reading, and to use such opportunities to give yourself as much exposure as possible.

Rapport is especially important for engaging assistance of the sort described above. Almost invariably, whoever actually assists you in collating and interpreting agency data will see himself as "doing you a favor", regardless of how insistent his superiors have been that he make his services freely and generously available to you. As part of the conditions for such a "favor,"

---

7. See, for instance, the superb paper by anthropologist Rosalie Hankey Wax, "Reciprocity in Field Work," in Richard N. Adams and Jack J. Preiss, eds., *Human Organization Research*, Dorsey Press, Homewood, Illinois, 1960, 90-98. Also see in Adams and Preiss the illuminating chapter by Joseph R. Gusfield, "Field Work Reciprocities in Studying a Social Movement," pp. 99-108.

you must reciprocate with expressions of gratitude and sympathy for his "going out of his way."

Another case in which the objects of one's research provide active assistance is in feeding unsolicited tips and leads or other types of information. This does not happen often, but when it does it can be most helpful. A cooperative informant might mail you a copy of a speech he has recently given, knowing that it will be of interest to you. Or he might see to it that you are put on the list of invitees to a banquet at which you will be able to meet a number of potential informants in an informal setting. To a certain extent, this sort of assistance can be encouraged simply by letting people know that it will be welcomed. It can be facilitated by having a telephone number and address where you can be reached or where messages can be left. It may even be useful to have business cards printed with this information. Relative to other research expenses this one is quite small and can return high dividends.

C. Exhausting access

Access can be exhausted, too, not just cultivated and built up. Whereas in some cases repeated exposure helps the researcher build rapport, in others exposure simply tears it down. In the extreme instance of the latter, one exposure is all the relationship will bear; this commonly occurs when the informant is defensive or antagonistic, or when he is extremely busy and cannot easily be imposed upon. Other instances are intermediate: the informant is willing to grant two but not three interviews—or three but not four. When access to an informant can be exhausted relatively quickly, it is generally wise to defer interviewing him until relatively late in the research; principally because the researcher's subsequently accumulated knowledge puts him in a better position to interview such an informant.

Usually, deferring interviews with such informants inflicts no hardship on the researcher, since the earliest stages of the interviewing research can be conducted by talking with the legion of lower-level officials and administrative assistants, public relations officer, etc. A very rich information source is to be found in retired officials and in agency officials who are part of a dissident faction.[8] These are rich sources at any time but are especially valuable in the earlier stages of research when it is thought advantageous to defer approaches to more highly-placed figures in the political establishment.

The researcher's reputation is also susceptible to being exhausted. It is perhaps not in danger of being lost, strictly speaking, so much as it is vulnerable to being transformed into an unwanted and detrimental reputation. Instead of being thought of as fair-minded, discreet, intelligent, and self-possessed, one can get the reputation of being partisan, a tale-bearer, a dope, or a dupe. The best way to avoid such an undesirable reputation is to eschew partisanship, indiscretion and, as we have already indicated, to actually be intelligent and self-possessed.

IV. Acquiring and using leverage

Political research, in its completed form, becomes a political resource. Whatever its merits or demerits as a piece of rational analysis, it becomes more than that. It becomes a justification for certain parties to attack others or defend themselves against attack, hence a weapon of persuasion in a war of propaganda.

---

8. My colleague William Niskanen relates that colonels twice passed over for promotion to general were a favored source for civilian policy analysts like himself in the Defense Department.

Although the tone and format of published policy research are typically neutral and disinterested, everyone recognizes that the research may be and often is used for political purposes, either by the author or by others. Hence informants are highly sensitive to the political implications of whatever they tell you. How an informant treats you depends in large part on how he thinks your work will be brought to bear on his personal or political interests.

Being wary of the possible political implications of what they might reveal, informants may be reluctant to talk freely and honestly. The researcher initially does well to assume that all interviewees confront this problem, even though it may not be known to what degree. In the more extreme cases it may be necessary to use leverage against the interviewee of various and subtle kinds. Before we turn to the problem in its most severe manifestations, though, let us set forth a basic strategy for conducting policy research interviews in general.[9]

A. Energy plus direction equals information

The interview is a process of interaction carried on between the informant and the researcher. The principal source of energy for this process should come from the informant, not the researcher. The latter should stimulate the former to talk and to keep on talking; and

---

9. It is probably a good idea to consult a few of the many social science guides to interviewing. A standard work, and a useful place to begin is: Charles F. Cannell and Robert L. Kahn, "Interviewing," in Gardner Lindzey and Elliot Aronson, eds., *The Handbook of Social Psychology*, 2nd ed., 1968, vol. 2, pp. 526-595. An extraordinarily rich and perceptive guide is that by Lewis Anthony Dexter, *Elite and Specialized Interviewing*, Evanston, Illinois: Northwestern University Press, 1970.

once a suitable momentum has been attained the researcher's role should then be to steer, to re-direct, to slow down, and to cross-examine. This procedure should give the informant a feeling that he has some power to define the situation and control the interview process—which he certainly does—a feeling which makes him more comfortable in speaking his mind.

Although the exact means to stimulate the informant are quite various, the presumed political significance of the research provides some clues as to how generally to proceed. You may be able to assist the informant to see in the research a vehicle of favorable public relations for himself or for some institution or cause with which he is associated. It is safe to say that most politicians, administrators, and important staff feel that much of their best and most valuable work is done behind the scenes and therefore does not come to the attention of those constituencies which would otherwise express appropriate appreciation. They are often correct in this assumption, and in the corollary assumption that the researcher and the research product may make their good works visible and earn the appreciation to which they are entitled.

A related but distinguishable motive for an informant to talk expansively is to "tell his side of the story." Whereas the public relations motive connotes a positive, or affirmative, attitude, telling one's side of the story is more defensive. The informant's implicit assumption here is that relevant constituencies are critical of his or his agency's conduct or policy, and that false or misleading or insufficient information is in some degree responsible for this situation. He might hope to correct the situation by expostulating aggressively, trying to put information in its "proper" perspective, or by clarifying and interpreting information which is already public. Hence he might welcome the researcher as someone who will be a vehicle for his opinions and information. At the very least, he might see the researcher as someone who will "put on the record" what he has to say, even if the researcher himself should prove to be unsympathetic. Ordinarily, the informant's goals in this respect are not incompatible with those of the researcher, and there will be no reasons why the researcher could not energize the informant's discussion by holding forth this promise of getting him on the record. Of course, the researcher must take pains to indicate, usually in subtle ways, that he is fair-minded and also sufficiently knowledgeable and intelligent to be able to put the informant on the record responsibly and adequately.

In most social science research involving interviews, it is assumed that the interviewer ought, as much as possible, to be a neutral instrument recording data emitted by the respondent. In general, this is an inappropriate model for policy research interviews. The informant assumes that the researcher is anything but a neutral instrument, since the whole object of the researcher's work is to arrive at some policy recommendations; and it is foolish for the researcher to try to appear in such an ill-fitting disguise. Thus the researcher need not fear to probe the informant with provocative and even argumentative questions or comments. These cause an informant to sharpen his wits and tone up his memory, and may raise his psychic metabolism sufficiently to infuse energy into the whole interview process. If done with proper finesse, the informant will appreciate the stimulation. The researcher's finesse, of course, consists of his being argumentative without sounding, or being, closed-minded or hostile. It is a good idea to broach argumentative remarks in such a way that the informant can retreat gracefully from the topic at hand into another topic, should he wish to do so, thus keeping the energy level up rather than dropping into an embarrassed taciturnity.

Most interviews will be conducted in the informant's office or place of work. Sometimes, however, a more informal setting should be arranged, such as a restaurant or bar. The method of note-taking should be compatible with such an informal setting, perhaps the back of an envelope handily stored in one's pocket for just such occasions.

Apart from energizing the informant, the interviewer's other main function in the interview process is to steer the informant onto topics of interest to the researcher himself (although unexpectedly interesting material often does turn up when the informant is allowed to take the lead completely for a while). How can this be done? First, it is necessary to interfere in the informant's conversation stream simply in order to reestablish the researcher's right to speak and also to temporarily slow the informant down without making him lose too much momentum. This can be done by interrupting with a short string of easily answered factual questions pertaining to the subject matter previously under discussion. The content of these questions, or at least the last one in the string, should be such as to work a transition to the next topic the researcher has in mind. Suppose, for example, that you are interviewing the Model Cities Coordinator in your city and he is telling you about his agency's relations with the mayor. You have heard enough on this subject and you now want to steer him onto his agency's current budget request to HUD. The conversation might go like this:

Informant: ...so you see we've had a devil of a fight with the mayor all the way. Maybe it's not his fault, of course, the city council being so conservative and the mayor needing support for his reelection....

A Handbook for Practice

Researcher: [Interrupting] Yes, he is up for reelection this year, isn't he?

Informant: Yes.

Researcher: Well at least he doesn't control your budget, does he?

Informant: True enough.

Researcher: But HUD does... and how are your relations with them? Do you get pretty much what you ask for from them, in the way of a budget, I mean?

The point is not to disguise from the informant the fact that you are trying to steer him away from one topic and onto another, although sometimes this is desirable and should be attempted. The point is really to help him move from one topic to another without his having to lose momentum or to feel awkward. Indeed, he will sometimes feel trapped on a topic which he himself would prefer to leave, and your job at such moments is to help him maneuver off the subject. If you cannot think of where you wish to lead him next, just think of a subject which is, at least, not implausible and which is not too demanding emotionally or intellectually. While you go in slow motion through that topic, both you and the informant will have a chance to collect your thoughts and feelings preparatory to moving to the next matter of serious concern.

Involving the informant in discussions of personalities is typically a matter of some delicacy. Above all, the informant must be reassured that you are not turning the interview into a gossip session: that he is not a purveyor of gossip, and you are not a seeker of it. This can be done by first introducing the name of the personality in a neutral, usually factual, context:

Researcher: A few moments ago you mentioned the Southside Community Health League. Dr. Green has been head of that for about a year now—or is it two?

Informant: Probably closer to two.

Researcher: Maybe it just seems shorter because I remember Dr. Black, his predecessor, so vividly.

Informant: Yes, Black was quite a leader there.

Researcher: Seems people have been more critical of Green—though I have heard quite complimentary things from some sources.

Informant: Yes, he's pretty controversial. He's certainly a competent administrator and been pretty nice to us—though we deal mainly with his deputy, Mr. White.

Researcher: How come?

Thus the conversation is turned to personalities by a sequence of small steps, in which each participant encourages the other and in which both assume responsibility for whatever gossipy quality may eventually threaten to intrude. Since personalities are such a sensitive topic, it is even a good idea for the researcher to sprinkle his conversation with allusions to people about whom he may have no desire to question the informant. When the researcher does desire to pursue a discussion of a particular personality, this procedure makes the discussion seem less of a departure from the normal course of topics.

Of course, if the informant has unpleasant things to say about the personality under discussion, the researcher might take pains to indicate his social, personal, and political distance from the individual. In the above excerpt, for example, the researcher has referred to "Dr. Green" and has indicated his distance by suggesting his unfamiliarity with certain particulars of Green's career. A contrary course might be followed if the informant has flattering things to say about the individual in question, though it is always a little risky to appear very close to anybody lest it arouse suspicions of partiality about the researcher.

B. The defensive informant

Occasionally one encounters an informant who is irrevocably committed to a defensive posture, for whom "no comment" is the primary defense and calculated evasion is the fallback position. It is desirable to diagnose this problem very early in the interview and to reassess one's goals for the interview in the light of this situation. The researcher should concentrate on gaining information about specific questions which this informant is able to answer but which are probably not answerable by any other source. Since so much of the researcher's energies will have to go into the cracking of the informant's defenses, it is wise to concentrate them on very specific objectives. Once these are in mind, one should begin to probe for them right away.

Once all these preliminary assessments are out of the way, and the interview has turned to specifics, the use of leverage is in order. First, let the informant understand as quickly as possible that you are aware of his defensive posture, and signal that you do not intend to be put off by it. You might try to communicate that his defensiveness will not help him, that you know too much already to be shunted aside, that you have access to other sources who have already told you much and to still others who are willing to tell you more. Indicate that these may be more prejudicial to his interests than his own revelations would be, and that he therefore has nothing to lose, and perhaps something to gain, by honest answers. A certain

amount of bluffing is sometimes possible and necessary, though to be sure there are obvious risks in this
tactic. It is always better to actually know as much as
you pretend to know, and to have access to the sources
you claim to have access to, than merely to bluff. Here
is a sample of such an interview, with the head of a
prominent local insurance company whom the researcher is pressing hard:

Researcher: One thing I'd like to get more information about is the problem insurance companies have
writing policies for merchants in so-called ghetto areas.

Informant: [Silence. Pause.]

Researcher: I mean, there may be problems because
these policies are risky business propositions.

Informant: [Silence. Pause.]

Researcher: People say they are risky, anyway. Do
underwriters in this area consider them risky?

Informant: I can't really say for sure.

Researcher: Well, some people in the Black Merchants Association claim that insurance companies
won't write policies for them at all, that they've been
classed as "unacceptable risks."

Informant: I don't really know... insurance writing is
the science of risks, isn't it?

Researcher: [Decides that informant will provide no
information on insurance industry doctrines or practices in general, or on the local underwriters in particular. Guesses that informant will be unwilling to discuss
the doctrines, or rules, applied by his own company,
and that he should therefore concentrate solely on
gathering information about the practices of informant's company.] Perhaps I can clarify my question by
being more concrete. In your own Bedrock Casualty

Company, are applicants ever turned down because they are thought to be unacceptable risks?

Informant: I can't say for sure. I'm not that close to the operating details of our very large company.

Researcher: Of course. [To signal he will not be put off:] You, or perhaps your secretary, could arrange for me to talk to someone at that level, though, couldn't you? [Seeking a different leverage point:] But tell me about the category of "unacceptable risks," does Bedrock Casualty tell its salesmen that the company will insure any premises provided the insured pays a high enough premium? [Shifting the terms of the question to throw informant off guard:] Or is there a limit on how high a premium the company will set?

Informant: Well, we do not like to charge exorbitant premiums, of course....

Researcher: [Interrupting] So within the existing limits on premiums there might in fact be businesses too risky to insure—hence "unacceptable?" [Holding to offensive:] How about cancellations? Has Bedrock cancelled or refused to renew any policies of ghetto merchants even though they have not filed any claims recently? This is another thing the Black Merchants Association has been complaining about.

Informant: [Deciding researcher knows more than he had thought and deciding to get preemptive protection against the Black Merchants Association's allegations:] Well, yes, we have cancelled a few, in the more riot-prone areas, and refused to renew other policies in that area. We had no choice; we stood to lose a lot of money in case of any trouble.

Researcher: [Graciously ignoring this "confession," and trying to induce informant to tell his side of the story:] Of course, that's quite understandable. I think most people recognize this problem. [Now taking aim on a single statistic, the proportion of all Bedrock policies in ghetto neighborhoods cancelled or not renewed in the last two years.] In the past, have you written many policies in that area?

Informant: Yes, we've done quite a bit, in the past anyway.

Researcher: You still do insure some business over there, don't you?

Informant: Yes, we do, though as I say, I'm not too close to the operating details....

Researcher: [Interrupting] Could you estimate what proportion of your policy holders from, say, two years ago you continue to insure? Is it eighty percent, twenty percent? Just to give me some rough idea.

Informant: Well, it would certainly be a lot closer to eighty than twenty but I really don't know.

Researcher: [Deciding that this would be an interesting datum and that it is worth pursuing vigorously:] Can we find out?

Informant: Not easily, It's not in any files anywhere in that form, and it would be awfully difficult to find out.

Researcher: [Not believing that it would be very difficult, and deciding that he is willing to contribute his own labor in searching the files, if necessary, resorts to a bluff:] People have the impression that Bedrock is less inclined to write policies for ghetto merchants than other companies in this area. I don't know where the facts come from—but I think some lawyers connected with the Black Merchants Association have been looking into legal aspects....

Informant: What? I'm sure we are no worse, or different, than any other company in town! I'd like to see these so-called facts!

Researcher: If I get any further clarification on that, I'd be happy to let you know. Meanwhile, I'd be willing to help out in whatever way you like in getting this information together concerning your own company's record in this field.

We interrupt this scene without a conclusion because, however it turns out, the researcher has done the best he could. The president of Bedrock Casualty may deliver the sought for information, or he may not. Good interviewing strategy and tactics do not guarantee success, especially when the odds are weighted against you to begin with.[10]

One common ploy used by a defensive informant is to reel out masses of irrelevant statistics and facts. These can easily swamp a naively data-worshipping researcher. Another ploy is to ramble garrulously about side issues, meanwhile running out the clock on whatever time limit he has set for the interview. The researcher's best defense against these ploys is to be able to recognize them for what they are.

If your own leverage fails, and if certain information is sufficiently important to you, you may be able to use someone else's. A graduate student researcher based in the university may have little leverage with determinedly defensive bureaucrats, for instance, but a legislator, or his staff assistant, will almost certainly have more. Hence, as a last resort, the student might per-

---

10. The researcher's bluffing tactic in this scene is of questionable morality. Although I believe it would be unethical in most circumstances, I think there are indeed occasions when it would be justified.

suade a sympathetic legislator to help out. Sometimes a newspaperman might be of assistance. Perhaps an established group can help. The local medical society, for example, might be able to get information from the county hospital administrator about hospital policies which no academic researcher, and possibly not even a county supervisor, could get.[11]

A significant constraint in using leverage is the desirability of maintaining cordial relations with whatever agency or individual is being pried apart. The researcher runs a clear risk of alienating the objects of his leverage tactics. With respect to a given study, this problem can be mitigated by postponing the more offensive tactics until relatively late, when the study is less vulnerable to being undermined by the offended party. The problem is more difficult, however, when the researcher envisions a long-term relationship with the agency or individual under scrutiny, one lasting well beyond the conclusion of the present research effort. In such cases, no doubt, certain information will have to be sacrificed in order to preserve a modicum of good will for the future.

V. Protecting Credibility

Like social science research, policy research is eventually subject to criticism on intellectual grounds. But unlike social science research, it is much more vulnerable on political grounds and, indeed, vulnerable to

---

11. Under certain conditions (probably quite uncommon) "freedom of information" laws can be utilized. As one policy researcher put it, "Consulting a lawyer is a necessity; having one ready to go to court, highly desirable. Convincing the bureaucrats that you know your rights is as important as showing them you know your subject." (John Mendeloff, personal communication.)

attack by the very subjects of the study. In social science research the subjects rarely become significant critics of the product, but in policy research their criticism is inevitable.[12] Therefore, the researcher should take steps to protect the ultimate political credibility of his work from politically motivated as well as from strictly intellectual attack.

A. Policy research aims at approximate truths

In contrast to social science research, the primary goal of policy research is not intellectual enlightenment (either for the researcher or for his professional colleagues), though enlightenment is inevitably a by-product. The goal, as we have said, is: to improve one's understanding of the policy problem, and of possible means of coping with it, to the point where it is possible responsibly to advocate a course of action. Thus policy research takes aim at broad and complex phenomena and is typically satisfied by very gross approximations of "truth," in contrast with social science research, which typically seeks more refined interpretations of narrowly circumscribed problems.[13] The gross and approximate character of policy research is an open invitation to politically inspired criticism. How can the researcher protect himself?

---

12. From both the researcher's and the politician's point of view, such criticism may be desirable. It will perhaps reveal significant but correctable mistakes of an analytical nature; and it will certainly reveal something about the nature, scope, and intensity of the political interests who will have to be taken into account.

13. Circumscription is necessary, of course, and it is "too narrow" only from the perspective of policy research. Narrow definition of a problem is often quite desirable in the context of social science research, which exploits the benefits of slowly accumulating reliable, if small, pieces of knowledge.

For one thing, he should make an attempt at touching base with anyone (or any institutional interest) who might later try to undermine the report by claiming to have been ignored. Indeed, it is a good idea to preempt such claims by quoting the party in the report, as evidence of a sort that the party's views were taken into account. For instance, if you are going to recommend alterations in the way superintendents are selected in a given school district, it would be best to interview representatives from the local association of school administrators and from the local chapters of the National Education Association and from the American Federation of Teachers. Spokesmen for these groups may have interesting opinions to contribute to the research project; but even if they do not, by consulting them the researcher gains protection against their criticisms should they decide to oppose the recommendations in his report. It may even be useful to send out a preliminary copy to these interests for reviews.

Secondly, one should seek out "experts" or others with political or intellectual authority to whom to attribute views, opinions, estimates, etc., about which the researcher feels especially uncertain. Quoting published sources is one way of making such attributions; and quotations from interviews is another. In addition, the researcher should plan to have experts lined up who will be willing to speak up in support of his work once it becomes public. If people are quoted in the report as having a view on this or that, they become natural targets for inquiring newspapermen or political decision-makers, to whom they also have an incentive to defend their quoted views.

Thirdly, the researcher should pay special attention to potential opponents and identify which propositions they are likely to attack. These should be bolstered by expert quotations in advance and a polite reference made to the existence of counter-arguments without at the same time giving them too much space or prominence. The very opponents who can be projected to raise these objections subsequently should be quoted, in order to defuse their claims that their arguments or positions were ignored. (There may be additional psychological advantages to the balanced or two-sided presentation, in terms sheerly of propaganda and persuasion directed at the reader.)

Statistical data are often useful for buttressing credibility. Used for this purpose, statistics play a documentation rather than an information role. They are used to document the validity of generalizations which political opponents might otherwise criticize, even though their truth were abundantly evident through more impressionistic sources. It is one thing to assert, for instance, that "we are experiencing a galloping inflation", and another to assert that "inflation is occurring at an annual rate of 5.5%."

B. Policy research is necessarily conjectural

Policy research has a special intellectual dimension which is unknown to social science research and which gives it an added dimension of intellectual and therefore political vulnerability. This dimension is that it conjectures about the future. It says in effect, adopt such-and-such policy and the probable result will be such-and-such. Now, the future is inherently uncertain, and the methods for conjecturing about it are underdeveloped and unreliable. Who can be certain that more police in neighborhood Y will decrease crime, or that manpower programs in city X will diminish unemployment? Even if it could be demonstrated— which it rarely can—that such policies led to these results in a dozen cities and neighborhoods across the land, one could not say for certain that city X and neighborhood Y would reap similar blessings.[14]

The good social science researcher makes no bones about the degree of uncertainty in his estimates of past and present conditions and rarely conjectures at length about the future. Indeed, it is considered good practice in social science research to err on the "conservative" side, to ascribe even greater uncertainty to one's conclusions than the researcher may feel subjectively. It is customary, for instance, to reject (at least *pro forma*) an hypothesis if there is more than a 5% chance that it could be in error as measured by standard tests of statistical significance.

Social scientific conservatism is a luxury which policy research cannot afford. No one suffers much if certain hypotheses in social science research are rejected even though they are in fact true. But if concentrated police effort in neighborhood Y actually would decrease crimes of violence substantially, any delays in implementing that policy in favor of "time for further study" are clearly a burden on the residents of neighborhood Y.

The policy researcher generally should not advocate a policy with any more (or less) confidence than he actually feels in it. Ordinarily this means that he will be a cautious advocate. It does not, however, mean he should acknowledge the superiority of the status quo— which, after all, is also a policy. The status quo imposes its own costs and benefits. It is up to the policy researcher to point them out and, more importantly, to force its defenders to be explicit in arguing that the costs of the status quo are probably less than those associated with the recommended alternative

---

14. See an excellent elaboration of this point in Paul E. Meehl (1971).

policy and/or that the benefits are greater.[15] A useful way of forcing this perspective on potential consumers of policy research is to list in the published report, as one of the proffered array of policy alternatives, "Continue Present Policies."

C. The risks of premature exposure

Politicians and policy researchers work on different timetables. Not infrequently the former call for "results" well before the research is in any sense finished. Even if no one demands results, moreover, unexpected opportunities do present themselves from the time when the researcher will wish his work were in a more finished state so that he could seize the auspicious moment to present the results.

One possible strategy, of course, is to map out (as much as possible) the timetable of potential political demands and to arrange your research timetable in at least partial correspondence.

An additional strategy is to prepare yourself as quickly as possible with answers to the crudest kinds of questions that might be asked of you. Since these are generally the kinds of answers politicians need and want anyway, you might as well have them early in the course of research as late.

Finally, it is important to line up your supporting experts early, as well as to touch base with potential opponents. Since, once again, these contacts must be

---

15. One of the benefits of the status quo is that it is not uncertain, and one of the costs of change is that the new policy may preempt the possibilities of adopting even better policies in the future. There is no reason not to include these assessments in the calculation of comparative costs and benefits.

made eventually, there is good reason to make them early rather than late.

D. Policy research asks for trouble

If he is asking for changes in policy which would substantially affect administrative and organizational routines, the good policy researcher will wish to make provisions for an orderly transition. Indeed, without assurances that such a transition is possible, administrators have an incentive—and a rhetorical weapon—to damage the proposed changes politically. Precisely because administrators are so wary of great disorder, they are reluctant to disclose to the researcher even the information he would use to plan a transition entailing minor disorder. Another difficulty in getting this information is the very large number of potential administrative trouble spots.

One device useful for collecting such information is the "limited circulation preliminary report." This sort of document can force people to take seriously the prospect of your work having an impact on them. They thereby develop a stake in making that impact as benign as possible. Their reactions to your "preliminary report" will be cantankerous, to be sure, for they will now point out all the deficiencies you would have wanted to learn about earlier—had they only been willing to take you seriously earlier! In order to put out an effective preliminary report, the researcher will need to have acquired enough political and intellectual credibility so that he can afford to lose some in the eyes of just such a cantankerous audience.[16]

---

16. See Bardach, *op. cit.*, pp. 216-218.

VI. Strategic dilemmas of policy research

By way of summary, and in order to introduce our final section in this brief essay on strategies of data-gathering in policy research, let us consider the question, which informants should be approached when? We may divide the "when" part of the question into "relatively early" and "relatively late" in the course of the research project.

Approach relatively early:

1) Persons who are likely to facilitate your search for rich information sources.

2) Powerful persons who directly or by your reputed connection with them will facilitate your access to sources.

3) Knowledgeable persons, who will provide you with the information you need to hedge against premature political exposure of your work, and whose information will contribute to your capacity to exert leverage against defensive interviewees.

4) Friendly experts, who will contribute to your political credibility in case of premature political exposure.

5) Potential opponents, with whom you touch base in order to hedge against premature political exposure.

Approach relatively late:

1) Hostile or defensive informants against whose tactics a prior build-up of leverage is desirable.

2) Busy informants, to whom you might lose access permanently once you have seen them and about whom you are not sufficiently informed to interview early.

3) Potential opponents, especially if powerful, who might try to ruin access to others and thereby cripple your research efforts.

4) Administrators who have knowledge of potential trouble spots but who will be unwilling to point them out until it appears to be in their self-interest.

There is one obvious contradiction between these two lists (approach potential opponents early and late) and several others which are not quite so obvious. Often it is the busy and the defensive informants who are also in the best position to facilitate the search for sources, open doors, and provide useful information. Top agency administrators, for instance, have plentiful experience with the policy problem under investigation and can provide easy access to sources, but they also have a vested interest in maintaining the status quo or something very close to it. In any event, they may not take kindly to having their activities scrutinized too carefully by an outsider. Other similar examples can easily be called to mind. There is in principle no way to reconcile these incompatible prescriptions of whom to approach early and whom late. The researcher will have to consider the full details of his particular situation and then balance the risks and rewards inherent in any given choice. There is no way of avoiding such tradeoffs, and the skilled policy researcher should simply make them consciously rather than inadvertently.

References

Bardach, Eugene (1972). *The Skill Factor in Politics: Repealing the Mental Commitment Laws in California.* University of California Press, Berkeley.

Cannell, Charles F. and Robert L. Kahn (1968). Interviewing. In G. Lindzey and E. Aronson (Eds.), *The Handbook of Social Psychology,* vol. 2, 526-595, 2nd ed. Addison-Wesley, Reading, Mass.

Charnley, Mitchell V. (1966). *Reporting.* 2nd ed. Holt, Rinehart and Winston, New York.

Dexter, Lewis A. (1970). *Elite and Specialized Interviewing.* Northwestern University Press, Evanston, Illinois.

Grubert, Harry (1971). How much do agencies know about error structure? In Report of the President's Commission on Federal Statistics, *Federal Statistics,* **2**, pp. 297-334. Government Printing Office, Washington, D.C.

Gusfield, Joseph R. (1960). Field work reciprocities in studying a social movement. In R. N. Adams and J. J. Preiss (Eds.), *Human Organization Research,* pp. 99-108. Dorsey Press, Homewood, Illinois.

Meehl, Paul E. (1971). Law and the fireside inductions: Some reflections of a clinical psychologist. In *The Journal of Social Issues,* **27:4**, 65-100.

Meltsner, Arnold (1972). Political feasibility and policy analysis. In *Public Administration Review,* Nov./Dec. 1972 pp. 859-867.

Wax, Rosalie H. (1960). Reciprocity in field work. In R. N. Adams and J. J. Preiss (Eds.) *Human Organization Research,* pp. 90-98. Dorsey Press, Homewood, Illinois.